THE
SHAKER COOKBOOK

THE
SHAKER
COOKBOOK

Not by Bread Alone

BY

CAROLINE B. PIERCY

ILLUSTRATED BY VIRGINIA FILSON WALSH

WEATHERVANE BOOKS

NEW YORK

This 1986 edition is published by Weathervane Books, distributed by Crown Publishers, Inc., 225 Park Avenue South, New York, New York 10003, by arrangement with Crown Publishers, Inc.

Printed and Bound in the United States of America

Library of Congress Cataloging-in-Publication Data

Piercy, Caroline B. (Caroline Behlen), 1886–1955.
  The Shaker cookbook.

  Previously published as: The Shaker cook book. 1953.
  Includes index.
  1. Cookery, Shaker. I. Title.
TX715.P62 1986   641.5′088288   86-10993

ISBN 0-517-62243-2

h g f e d c b a

To the great host of Shaker "Kitchen Sisters" who
labored to please God in preparing the
viands entrusted to their hands

I AM DEEPLY GRATEFUL

To the little old cook book containing the Shaker recipes gleaned by my mother, for to it I owe my genuine interest in all things Shaker;

To the Western Reserve Historical Society Librarians who have set before me abundant material in the form of Shaker household journals, travel records and diaries which have given me intimate glimpses into the everyday life at North Union;

To Mrs. Jessie Haynes, of the Wayside Museums of Harvard, Massachusetts, who sent me old Shaker recipes from Canterbury Community;

To Sister Ethel Peacock, of Sabbathday Lake Shakers, who enlightened me on the subject of Shaker Applesauce and Bread-making;

To Sister Mildred Barker, of Sabbathday Lake Shakers, for some recipes of sweetmeats for which that Community is still famous—such chocolate mints! such preserves!

To Sister Marguerite Frost, of Canterbury Community, who has most generously furnished me material on Shaker Herb Culture and some very flavorful recipes;

To Mrs. Julius Zieget, of Peterboro, New Hampshire, and of Philadelphia, who introduced me to Sister Marguerite and also to her New England herb garden;

To Sister Jennie Wells, of Hancock Community in Massachusettes, for her far-famed rule for "Shaker potatoes";

To Mr. William Harrison, director of the Wayside Museums, for his reference to "The Story of the Shakers and Some of Their Cooking Recipes—Calendar for 1882-3," and to my doctor-husband who so patiently let me "try out" on him many of these dishes and who gave me invaluable pointers on nutrition—"the basic seven," calories, vitamins and minerals—and on the international or world-wide important position food holds today.

CONTENTS

THE
SHAKER COOKBOOK

A FORETASTE

This little volume on Shaker cookery may never find its way into the technology departments of our large libraries where cookbooks stand in neat rows by the legion, for I am writing it not for its scientific contribution, but rather to set forth the Shakers' important contributions to the development of an all-American cookery when our land was yet young.

I was asked to prepare a booklet on Shaker cookery for the Shaker Historical Society of Cleveland, Ohio. As I delved into the subject, I became fascinated by the project, not only because many of the recipes were unique and deserved preservation, but chiefly because of the attitude of this religious order toward food and its preparation—which is an inspiring bit of Americana worthy of consideration at a time when the vast problem of food and nutrition is of vital world interest. According to the Shaker belief, work and worship are intricately intertwined: "Give your hands to work and your heart to God" was their well-known motto. It is by the fruits of their labor that they became known as craftsmen of great skill and complete honesty.

To the Shakers, or Believers in Christ's Second Appearing, as they chose to call themselves, their sole purpose in life was to establish God's Kingdom here upon earth. Their hands, their minds, their hearts were wholly dedicated to that end, and therefore their vast kitchens and numerous workshops were as sacred to them as were their meeting houses and assembly halls. Here they put into concrete expression—into luscious pies, dumplings and dainty flummeries, or into wooden household utensils and fine skeins of yarn and flax—what their religion taught, that man was put into this world in order to establish "Heavens on earth" where universal peace, genuine brotherly love and complete honesty reigned.

For material for my booklet on Shaker cookery I turned

to a well-finger-marked manuscript cook book which along with several others stood on our pantry shelf when I was a very small child. This particular volume had always fascinated me; in fact, it would be more exact to say that for me it wore a halo or a lovely aura, for on its blue-lined pages were written in my mother's dainty Spencerian hand recipes for *Clymena Miner's Blue Flower Omelets, Sister Abigail's Strawberry Flummery* and *Sister Content's Rosemary and Other Herb Butters for Supper-sandwiches and Spreads on Freshly Cooked Vegetables.* Such mouth-watering suggestions! And there were many other neatly penned rules for making *Crunchy Sugar Cookies, Molasses Taffy, Sugared Rose Petals* and *Maple Creams* bulging with the rich meats of butternuts —each a sufficient reason for loving this manuscript volume on cookery; but what gave the little book its well-earned aura and special flavor was that whenever my mother and I used these time-honored recipes, she would tell me how she gleaned this rare collection. It all resulted from her many visits as a child and later as a young woman to the "Valley of God's Pleasure," commonly known as the North Union Shaker Community about a mile from her former home.

This peaceful community, she would tell me, "was without jail, without poor, without saloons, nor did they learn the art of war therein! These devout Shakers love one another as brothers and sisters. They have withdrawn from the world in order to establish villages throughout our young nation, where the Golden Rule is the one law by which they live. When their many tasks are completed, daily they gather at their meetings where they dance before the Lord for pure joy and gratitude for the countless good gifts He has bestowed upon His children and, also, in order to drive away any wrong thoughts or desires which may come to them."

How I longed to know these devout souls! How it stimulated my youthful imagination to think of the Sisters endlessly preparing delicious food for their enormous households, and not looking upon it as a labor, but as a glorious opportunity to serve God joyously by feeding his children! As we concocted a Shaker apple pie, delicately flavored with rose-water, from the pages of this enchanting cook book, my mother would tell me how her father had the timber and grain of their large acreage milled by the skilled Brethren; had their apples converted into the famed Shaker cider at their presses. There, also, her family bought their brooms, vats, barrels, kegs, firkins and noggins, wooden pails and mammoth washtubs. The butter, lard, cheese and eggs, as well as applesauce and other preserves this large family consumed, they bought from Deacon Daniel, the Shaker peddler who made his weekly rounds with a covered wagon crammed to the ribs with faultless Shaker produce.

It was in the Sisters' knitting-shed that this pioneer family bought the creamy-white and ruby-red yarns for the stockings, mittens, mufflers and fascinators needed throughout the long winters. Nor must we neglect mentioning the countless baskets they bought from the Believers, whose skilled fingers fashioned containers for every conceivable use from picking berries to gathering faggots in the nearby forest. There were wide, sturdy clothes baskets that held a dozen freshly tubbed sheets; cheese baskets always bleached white from the whey; and wee sewing baskets woven as smooth as velvet for specially fine needlecraft.

Here at these Shaker villages always steeped in a Sabbath quiet, my mother became acquainted with the excellency of Shaker cookery, for wide hospitality reigned in these "Kingdoms of God upon earth." Seldom was she allowed to leave North Union or The Valley of God's Pleasure without breaking bread—and such bread!—with some of the Sisters. Often times she would come away with one or many of the tried recipes, which she copied into the blue-lined pages of the above-mentioned cookbook. The little volume contained more than rules for lush, carefully prepared food. Its recipes were full-flavored with consecration and with a zeal for perfection, for whatever a Shaker undertook to accomplish she consecrated her entire being to its fulfilment. The Shaker's silent prayers were never interrupted with "amens," for they never ceased praying! Like their predecessors, the Quakers, these Shaking-Quakers constantly listened for the still, small voice and kept attuned to God for inspiration, guidance and revelation in whatever task they performed. Be it the making of a pie or herb-laden soufflé or the erecting of a house of worship, their hands were equally consecrated to the task and they never ceased to seek better ways and means of performing their allotted duties.

Who were these Shakers and whence came they? This religious sect originated about 1747 among a group of English Quakers who had been strongly influenced by a remnant of the French Prophets, or Camisards, who under persecution had fled France to the British Isles. Among this group who worshipped in Manchester, England, there arose a young woman, Ann Lee. She was the daughter of a blacksmith. Wholly illiterate, for there were no schools for the poor in England in her day, but possessing such an honest and consuming desire to know God and to do His will, she soon developed great spiritual power and insight, and was accepted as the second embodiment of the Christ spirit upon earth by the Shaking-Quakers. Her followers henceforth called her Mother Ann.

Great were the persecutions of these Shakers in England. In 1774 Mother Ann and seven of her followers came to America where it had been revealed to her they would re-establish the Apostolic Church. Arriving at the inopportune time of the outbreak of the American Revolution, this little band of unknown Britishers soon realized it was not the time to preach a new religion, especially one which violently decried war! In fact, they were looked upon as British spies and for six months were confined to prison.

It was in the closing years of the American Revolution, when at times it seemed as if almost nothing had been accomplished by five years of sacrifice, bloodshed and broken homes, that a religious revival broke forth on the New England frontier. The Colonies lacked religious leaders; what had become of the glorious faith of the founders of our land! Hundreds of war-weary souls were seeking a solution—were looking for salvation. Then word reached them that in the wilderness above Albany—in Niskayuna—dwelt a strange little band of Believers who were attempting to re-establish the Early Christian Church; they lived by the Golden Rule and patterned their lives wholly upon that of Jesus Christ, living celibate lives, sharing all they possessed, and being complete pacifists.

Thither the war-weary pilgrims traveled—by wagon, on foot and by horse; hundreds of them! None was turned away hungry. Thousands of converts soon joined the ranks of the Believers in Christ's Second Appearing, or Shakers.

Within ten years the original little band of English Shakers had gone to their rest.

The thousands of converts they had made were gathered into eleven Shaker Communities in Maine, New Hampshire, Connecticut, Massachusetts and New York. The organization of these communities was left entirely within American hands—in the hands of the Colonists who had just won their independence. Little by little these Shaker groups came into possession of land on which they erected dwellings, meeting houses, schools, blacksmith shops, barns and stables. Here into the common coffers of the communities each convert poured whatever he possessed—a feather-bed, a yoke of oxen, a fine farm or a couple of hens, whatever constituted his worldly possessions after his debts were paid. In Anna White's *Shakerism* we read: "The ingathering of souls became so numerous that great hopes were raised that the world would be redeemed by the Gospel revealed to them, and the cry went forth, 'Make room for thousands!' They gradually added building to building and fertile field to hill-top and valley. Cheerfully the Shakers bore the burden of all this heavy toil with their own hands; they ate scanty rations, denied themselves every luxury and wore coarse clothing so that the Kingdom might be made ready for the children who were yet to claim their inheritance."

All this happened in the early days of the Federal period —the most formative stage of our history. Adventure and experiment were the order of the day. Because of the bitter emnity against Britain, foreign dress, foods and wine were rapidly discarded to a large extent for native homespuns, home-brews and native ciders. The First Lady of the Land, Martha Washington, came to the fore and advocated the cultivation and development of an all-American Cookery! The federated Colonies, or States as they were now called, with almost unlimited resources of unturned sod and uncut virgin forests, had what seemed at the time an inexhaustible supply of game and wild foods. Again, the Colonists, upon arrival in this land, found many new foods awaiting them, such as Indian maize (corn), sweet potatoes, certain beans, pumpkins, squash, many new varieties of berries and wild plums and cranberries. All this profusion of new foods led to new dishes, new ways of cooking and a diet with a distinctive American flavor.

In this young nation teeming with activity—trying out this and that in an attempt to establish an independent American way of life, the Shakers played an important role. In the eleven Shaker communities, or model democracies, that had been formed, where many hands united, their village streets were soon lined with buildings of excellent architecture. These buildings were equipped with furniture of their own making, designed for utility and durability. Their fields were vast and well cultivated and their orchards and vineyards soon stretched off at great distances. Well-tilled vegetable and herb gardens skirted each kitchen where substantial meals for a hundred Brethren and Sisters were prepared thrice daily.

In the early 1800's, nineteen such Shaker communities were scattered from New England to Eastern Indiana. Customs and ideals were taking definite form. Because of the religious zeal and integrity of the Shakers, their communities throve remarkably and soon became models of thrift and high standards of living. These Shakers were thorough and exact in whatever they undertook, and they were ever seeking better ways and means of performing the Herculean tasks of clearing and cultivating the land and harvesting their vast crops—thus they became inventors and produced countless gadgets, tools and machinery to increase their efficiency in production. They invented a rotary harrow, a threshing machine, a fertilizer spreader, a splint-cutting machine for the manufacture of baskets and boxes, a better windmill, an improved wood-burning stove, a pea sheller, a butter churn driven by water power, a self-acting cheese press, an apple parer, a revolving oven and many other labor-saving devices. They seldom applied for patents on their inventions, for they considered such restrictions "as smacking of Monopoly" which was contrary to the Golden Rule.

Their various communities being under the leadership of Mt. Lebanon, New York, through constant communication and frequent visits all the communities shared in these improvements of field, factory and kitchen. Thus all their communities were soon in advance of their neighbors in production methods. The Shakers were also skilled horticulturists, developing new and better species of apples, plums and peaches. Moreover, they conducted the first nurseries in their localities. They were also pioneers in raising, packaging and distributing garden seeds in America. This called for scientific methods of selection from only the thriftiest plants. This distribution called for leaflets on how to plant the seeds and how to cook and prepare the food grown. Again, the Shakers carried on the first large-scale production of kitchen and medicinal herbs and widely distributed information concerning their proper use. They improved their herds and flocks by importing and breeding thoroughbred stock. They observed high standards of sanitation in their vast barns and dairies when bacteria were yet unheard of and milk was often dangerously infected by unsanitary conditions.

Moreover, the Believers applied almost scientific methods in their cooking, for in working with vast amounts of food, exact weights and measures and relative amounts had to be estimated and established, in a day when their contemporaries added "a dash of this and a glob of that" in making their favorite dishes. Cooking for a hundred hungry mouths thrice daily demanded definite rules and exact measurements. Again, the Shakers recorded the works of their hands and left us definite information on cookery in a day when books "on the Art of Cooking" were few. In 1796 *American Cookery or the Art of Dressing Viands, Fish and Vegetables and the Best Modes of Making Pastries, Puffs, Tarts, Custards and all kinds of Cakes from Imperial Plum to Plain Cake; Adapted to This Country and All Grades of Life,* by Amelia Simmons, An American Orphan, was published. Besides the title the book contained forty-six pages of detailed recipes, household hints and many home remedies. In 1829 another volume on American cookery appeared, entitled *The Frugal Housewife,* by Lydia Childs, which doled out ninety some pages of miscellaneous information.

In the large Shaker literature there is but one printed cookbook. This was written by Sister Mary Whitcher, and entitled *The Shaker Housekeeper*. However, in the manuscript annals of the various communities there are countless excellent recipes used by these pioneer Americans.

Another strong influence the Shakers had upon our national diet was that in the late 1830's a ban was placed upon the use of meat throughout Shakerdom, which lasted for twelve years. Green vegetables, fruits, cereals, eggs, cheese and dairy products were substituted at a time when heavy meat diets, salt pork and corn were the accepted foods of the day. It was at this period that due to lack of hostelries, the western Shaker Societies served thousands of meals to the hosts of Easterners who migrated west by the hundreds. Enticed by the abundance of good food and comfortable lodgings, many a western trek ended within the Shaker gates. "We came seeking food and shelter, kind Elder, never realizing that the gates of eternal salvation would be opened up to us," was the frequent reward for Shaker hospitality!

Another strong influence these communities had on American cooking in this formative period was that the Shaker societies were the orphanages of that day, and, one might say, they were the forerunner of the domestic science training schools of a later period, for every girl raised by the order received along with her book-learning a thorough education in housewifery. Elder Fredrick Evans, one of the Shakers' greatest spokesman, stated that hundreds of such Shaker-trained young women went forth into the world when they became of age, thoroughly equipped to conduct a well-run household.

Probably the farthest-reaching Shaker influence on American cookery was the fact that they were pioneers in the canning industry. The records show that they distributed thousands upon thousands of items of preserved food to

markets as far distant as New Orleans. Each item was carefully inspected and labeled before it passed beyond the
Shaker gates. The high standard of quality possessed by their
goods created a great demand among the public for Shaker
products. The Shaker label was a mark of their integrity on
any item which bore their name.

In a day when calories and vitamins were yet unheard
of, the Shaker sisters, because of their abhorrence of waste,
used their "pot-licker," water in which certain vegetables
had been cooked, in making gravies, stews and soups. Again,
they scrubbed their vegetables and usually boiled them in
their peels, a method which we know is approved of today,
for it conserves valuable nutrition. At their semi-weekly
social meetings, articles from the New York papers and from
science journals which pertained to agriculture and food and
any new light on hygiene were read and freely discussed.
Later, in 1871, the Shakers published their own magazine;
at first it was called *The Shaker* and then the *Manifesto*. A
special column entitled "Home Topics" contained recipes
and household hints. This magazine had a fairly wide distribution among "the World People" as well as among all
the Shaker communities. Again, the *Manifesto* had many
items about diet and its relation to health.

Another factor that contributed to Shaker food being
well prepared was that their great kitchens were built for
communal living and were equipped with conveniences often
years ahead of the times—running water, stone sinks, specially built ranges and ovens, such as the revolving pie oven
at Canterbury planned so that heat was evenly distributed
and the baked loaves and confections could most easily be
removed by rotating the oven shelves. Cleanliness was almost
a part of the Shaker creed. Mother Ann often remarked:
"There is no dirt or filth in Heaven," and since they strove
to establish "Heavens on Earth," these delightful communi-

ties were kept, as near as possible, spotless! The great kitchens and pantries were lined with innumerable cupboards and drawers "where everything had its place and was kept in its place" according to Mother Ann's wise admonitions. To add further to the efficiency of these kitchens there was always a cooking kitchen and a baking kitchen. In the high-ceilinged, well-ventilated cellar, close to the fruit and vegetable bins, was the canning kitchen especially equipped with great ranges, sufficient tables and tremendous copper kettles which could turn bushels of raw food into rare sauces and condiments for the long winter ahead. It was in these canning kitchens that American mass production first saw the light of day.

Like Shaker architecture, furniture and dress, the cooking expressed genuine simplicity and good quality. The Believers abhorred shoddy work, adulteration and useless ornamentation. All their work was colored and inspired by Mother Ann's simple truths, such as "Labor to make the ways of God your ways";—concerning cooking she advised the sisters: "See that your victuals are prepared in good order and on time so that when the Brethren return from their labors in the fields, they can bless you and eat their food with thankfulness, without murmuring, and thereafter be able to worship in the beauty of holiness."

The Sisters well realized that the planning, preparing and serving of meals was a tremendous responsibility and a great service to God, for on this task depended the health, comfort and well-being of the large families. The Brethren hungry from toil in the fields and workshop, the growing children from their small tasks, the aged Believers, all gathered about the long trestled tables thrice daily looking for sustenance, satisfaction and fellowship. It was this conviction, that in her hands had been placed a task into which she must put all the wisdom and skill with which God had endowed a Shaker woman, that earned for Shaker cookery the high praise from all who partook of their wholesome, delicious fare. These faithful laborers in the kitchen keenly realized that man does not live by bread alone! Their food was well seasoned with gratitude and consecration!

GENERAL INFORMATION

The recipes used in this volume in their original form called for enormous quantities. The Shaker "family," or basic unit of the various communities, consisted of from thirty to one hundred members—after that limit was reached, a new family was formed. Dwelling-houses, dining rooms and workshops were provided for each family. Consequently, the early recipes were scaled to meals for from thirty to one hundred hard workers.

These have been reduced from their original form to the usual-size recipe of today, and have been tested by the writer and not found wanting in interest and flavor—from the rosewater-flavored apple pie to the leg of lamb laved in hot butter with a bunch of freshly plucked rosemary.

All measurements are level.

Standard measuring utensils have been used. The original rules often called for a "teacup full" or a "large coffeecup full," but through trial and error and comparison with like recipes of today, correct measurements have been reached.

Correct temperatures, as stated, should be used.

Substitutions should not be used; any cook knows that there is no substitute for butter or cream when called for. Of these, the good Shakers had aplenty in the day when their board was renowned for its good and ample fare. Unsalted butter was used in cake-making. Also in buttering cake pans.

All-purpose flour is used in all recipes calling for flour except when otherwise stated.

Season all culinary attempts with Shaker patience, enthusiasm and with the Believers' joy of living!

Beverages

The subject of Shaker beverages is an important one, for these devout religionists were pioneers in the Temperance Movement in this country. In the early days, especially along the frontier, practically everyone washed down his vituals and slaked his thirst with alcoholic liquors, ranging from cider, beer and ale to rum and whiskies; the child of two, the "hired help," the teacher or the preacher thus quenched his thirst. At every husking bee, barn raisin' and social event "the little brown jug" made its merry rounds! In fact, the absolute abstainer was looked upon with suspicion and considered anti-social.

In rural areas heavy drinking was attributed to a great extent to the monotony of isolated living and the Herculean task of clearing and grubbing the land. Others held that the salt-meat diet of that day called for the use of liquor. The lack of roads made it impossible to market grains and fruits; therefore such bulky produce was reduced to liquids which were more easily transported and preserved. Practically every rural district had its distillery before it built a school or a church.

In those early days water and milk were not used as beverages. Water was a scarce item, for wells had to be dug and these were often located in the barnyard for convenience in watering the stock. This water soon became polluted, while the water of many rivers and streams was contaminated by the presence of Indian villages along the banks. Moreover, milk was scarce because cows were raised chiefly for their hides and for breeding the oxen, which were the work animals on the farms and were used in transportation. Again, very few persons drank milk, for there was a general impression in that day that it caused various diseases, which it probably did, since milk, a ready medium for the growth of bacteria, was then handled in a most unsanitary way—in open wooden containers—and was probably often highly contaminated. Glass milk bottles were not dreamed of until they appeared in Philadelphia in 1880.

Until the Shakers had ample herds, cider was their staple beverage. And what cider! Shaker cider was famous throughout the young nation!

In 1828 the head Shaker community at New Lebanon, New York, issued an edict prohibiting the use of all alcoholic beverages throughout Shakerdom. It read: "Hereafter beer, cider, wines and all ardent liquors are banned on all occasions; at house-raisings, husking-bees, harvestings and all other such gatherings. . . ." The far-famed Shaker cider was henceforth relegated to the vinegar barrel, to be used in salads, sauces and pickles, or boiled down and bottled for sauces on steam puddings or in making mince-meat or for "apple-sass."

Tea and coffee, both expensive imports, were very scarce at the frontier; by the time they had been transported across the mountains by pack horse, the price was prohibitive. Consequently all sorts of substitutes were used, such as black birch bark, spice bark, sassafras, mint, tanzy, camomile and redwood leaves in place of tea, while corn and other grains, peas, chicory root and the seeds of the locust trees were parched and used in place of coffee. Then in 1837 another edict was sent forth from the New Lebanon community prohibiting in all the Shaker communities the use of coffee and tea, meat and tobacco except by members over sixty years of age. We read that "this restriction brought about a tremendous spiritual awakening among the Believers, for they learned that temperance meant curbing all carnal appetites and that they must rely for their strength and inspiration upon God rather than upon some stimulant."

The records show that many a drunkard entered the Shaker gates, where nothing alcoholic was to be had, and after sharing in constructive labor and inspired by a strong faith in the perfectability of man, he regained complete control of his abnormal cravings.

SHAKER MULLED CIDER
3 QUARTS CIDER
1 TEASPOON WHOLE CLOVES (HEADS REMOVED)
1 WHOLE NUTMEG
1 STICK CINNAMON
1/2 CUP SUGAR

Put all ingredients in enameled pot and simmer for five minutes. Strain and serve very hot in warmed noggins (goblets). Serves 20.   Amelia's Shaker Recipes

The far-famed Shaker cider was made by selecting perfect apples (a late fall apple was preferred). "Place them on the grass on the north or shady side of the grain barn to mellow. When at thirty feet distance you catch the fragrant apple aroma, they are ready for the press," the rule states. Probably what made Shaker cider outstanding was the fact that they never dumped culls or tainted apples into their presses.

From the day the first New England apple orchards bore fruit (which was seven years after planting) cider was the most popular beverage Down East. This drink was cheap, costing but a few shillings a barrel. In Colonial days the thrifty farmer laid in a supply of from ten to thirty barrels of this thirst-quencher "against winter."

Cider-making is a very ancient and simple process. The juice was pressed from the crushed fruit, after which it was passed through a straw sieve and run off into barrels. The barrels were then placed in a cool cellar where, after the bung was removed, time and nature did the work.

After the Shakers advocated total abstinence, they pasteurized the sweet cider rather than use chemicals to prevent fermentation.

The ancient Hebrew word for cider is "Shakar." Augustine wrote on the goodness of taste and the health-giving properties of cider back in 325.

SHAKER COLD TEA

Use 1 teaspoon of good imported tea to a large tumbler of cold water. Use only glass or porcelain container and let stand for 12 hours. Strain and add ice. Sweeten to taste.

Tea made by this method will never "cloud," because the tannin is not drawn from the leaves. Made thus it has a delightful bouquet and the same stimulating effect as hot tea.

Amelia's Shaker Recipes

When the Shakers went a-picnicking at the Valley of God's Pleasure (North Union) they often took great crocks of this cold tea (made by the above method), and it was considered a delightful beverage by all who partook thereof.

When we learn that the tea plant belongs to the camellia family, we love its delicate taste and fragrance all the more. Historically, tea has played an important role in America. When in 1664 Queen Charlotte of England was presented with a gift of tea by the East India Company, she was so delighted with the beverage that it soon became a fashionable drink throughout the British Isles, and with increasing emigration, this British taste soon invaded our Colonies. It might have become our national beverage except for the tax placed on it, which resulted in the Boston Tea Party which led to the American Revolution.

SHAKER-STYLE LEMONADE

6 LEMONS
1 CUP SUGAR
1 CUP BOILING WATER
8 CUPS VERY COLD WATER

Roll the lemons well; cut in half and squeeze out juice. Strain and add sugar. Pour the boiling water over the lemon rinds and let stand until cold. Strain and add cold water to juice. The hot water extracts the oil from the rinds and thus adds greatly to the flavor. Add a little ice to each mug. Very refreshing for the sick and aged. Serves 6.

Sister Amelia, North Union

The Shakers greatly appreciated the lemon. They raised practically all their food, but considered lemons such a necessary part of their diet, that according to the old accounts lemons were the first food ever purchased by North Union. They used them in pies, custards, sauces and beverages.

Our North Union Shaker founders, having received their training in cooking Down East, undoubtedly were taught what an important role the humble little lemon had played in the history of colonization. The Merchant Shipping Act of 1667 stated that every British ship going to countries where lemons were not grown was required to take enough lemons or limes so that every member of the crew and every passenger had an ounce of citrus juice daily in order to ward off the frightful scourge of scurvy so prevalent in those days.

This valuable little citrus fruit was well known by the Greeks and the Romans. It was introduced into Spain in the twelfth century, where large orchards of lemons were planted and thence shipped to the Azores. Large quantities of this fruit were sent to the British Isles as early as the tenth century.

SHAKER LEMON BEER

4 LEMONS
4 CUPS SUGAR
1 POUND TARTARIC ACID (FROM DRUG STORE)
1 OUNCE GINGER ROOT
2 GALLONS BOILING WATER
1 CUP BEST HOMEMADE YEAST (2 CAKES COMPRESSED)

Roll the lemons until soft and cut paper thin. Add sugar, tartaric acid and ginger root. Then add the boiling water and let stand until tepid. Add yeast, and keep in warm place; let stand 6 hours. Strain. Then bottle and cork tightly. It will be ready to drink in 6 days, and will be found very refreshing.   South Union

30

The Shaker *Manifesto* (a monthly magazine published by the Shakers from 1871 to 1899) contained in its April, 1881, issue, a lengthy article on the virtues of lemons. Herein it is stated that "Lemonade is one of the healthiest and most refreshing drinks of all drinks; suitable for almost all stomach and bowel disorders and excellent in most sicknesses."

This same article recommended the use of lemons not only for their healthful properties but also as an excellent cleansing agent to be used on fingernails, as a rinse for hair when shampooing, and as a satisfactory mouth wash. Great was the Shakers' faith in lemons! They used quantities of them!

"Only the best of spring water should be used in making beverages. Set beverages in the spring-house or hang in well for several hours before using."—Sister Lisset

SHAKER GINGERADE

4 OUNCES GINGER ROOT
4 LEMONS
2 QUARTS BOILING WATER
2 CUPS LEMON JUICE
SUGAR SYRUP TO TASTE

Cut the ginger root into small pieces and add the lemon rind cut into paper-thin strips; pour the boiling water over this and let steep for 5 minutes. Strain, and when perfectly cold add lemon juice and sugar syrup to suit taste; some like it sweet and some like the tang of the lemon. Dilute with very cold water and chips of ice. In hot weather, sprigs of mint inserted in glasses add interest to this beverage. Serves 8.

Union Village

In the early 1800's there was a great vogue among the "World People" for visiting mineral springs where patients not only drank the water but bathed in it. Poland Springs, Maine, was one of the health resorts owned by the Rickers brothers. Both the Alfred and the New Glouchester (now Sabbathday Lake) Shakers exchanged mill rights with the Ricker brothers for the benefits of these waters.

In 1807 Dr. Phillip Physick of New England prepared carbonated waters which were supposed to contain some of the healing properties of the mineral spring water for his patients. These carbonated waters became tremendously popular. The Shakers at North Union made a "charged water" flavored with certain fruit juices, which they marketed very successfully. Other Shaker communities produced "sarsaparilla" and yet other "healing waters."

Syllabub: Sweeten a gallon of cider with crushed maple sugar. Do not stint on the sweetening! Grate a nutmeg on top. Then milk the cow into this mixture. Drink while warm and foamy. This is not a Shaker method of making this one-time famous drink!

SHAKER HERBADE

1/2 CUP LEMON BALM, CUT FINE
1/2 CUP MINT, CHOPPED FINE
1/2 **CUP REGULAR SUGAR SYRUP**
1/2 CUP LEMON JUICE
1/4 CUP ORANGE JUICE
4 QUARTS GINGER ALE (OR SHAKER GINGERADE, SEE ABOVE)

Combine the first five ingredients and let stand 1 hour. Then add the ginger ale or gingerade. Serves 16.

This is an old Shaker recipe used by the Canterbury community, and was given to Mrs. Julius Zieget of Peterboro, New Hampshire, where she has a delightful New England herb garden. Lemon balm, which the dictionary defines as a menthaceous plant of the genus Melissa, was widely cultivated as a garden herb and bee plant. Its leaves give off a lemony, minty aroma which has prompted the writer to put sprigs of it among her table linens.

SHAKER MINT CUP

2 CUPS TENDER MINT LEAVES, CUT FINE

2 CUPS SUGAR

2 CUPS WATER

JUST A DASH OF SALT

2 QUARTS OF GINGER ALE (OR SHAKER GINGERADE, SEE ABOVE)

Make a simple syrup by boiling the sugar and water 3 minutes. Add salt. Pour boiling syrup over the leaves. Let stand until cool. Strain. Then add ginger ale or gingerade. You will find the salt will help draw out the mint flavor from the leaves. Serve very cold. A sprig of mint helps pretty up this good drink. Serves 8.

Sister Mary Gass, Whitewater Shakers

SHAKER FRUIT SHRUB

2 QUARTS RED RASPBERRIES

1 CUP LEMON JUICE

1 1/2 CUPS SUGAR

2 QUARTS WATER

Make a thin syrup by boiling sugar and water 3 minutes.

Crush berries and pour hot syrup over fruit. Let stand until cool, and strain. Add lemon juice and a little ice. This is a delightful and refreshing drink. Strawberries, blackberries or black raspberries can be used in the same way. Serves 8.

Sister Lisset, North Union

The North Union Shakers were the first settlers in these parts to erect ice-houses and fill them with ice from their large lakes. The construction of these buildings was unique, for we read: "The double walls of the ice-house were packed with sawdust from their mill and the three-ply roof was filled with the same protection from the summer heat. The buildings was windowless. The stone floor was covered with hay and then with a layer of sawdust."

There is an old settler still living in these parts, who as a young man helped the Shakers cut ice on the now famous Shaker lakes of the Cleveland Park system. He tells in a most dramatic fashion how carefully the Shakers scraped all the snow from the surface before marking it into five-foot squares. He claims: "They saw to it that these markings were exactly straight and even. They never tolerated sloppy work of any kind!

"Very special curved saws carved the great cakes of ice from the frozen lakes. When a thaw or a snowstorm threatened the ice crop, we often worked late into the night harvesting what we could. When the ice-house was filled, we sealed her up until summer. If the weather was really cold, how our beards would hang with icicles!" was this old-timer's comment.

SHAKER APPLE DULCET

2 GLASSES APPLE JELLY
4 CUPS BOILING WATER
2 QUARTS BEST SHAKER CIDER
1 NUTMEG, GRATED
6 EGG WHITES
8 SPRIGS OF MINT

Whip the jelly to a froth by gradually beating in the boiling water. Cool and add cider; powder with nutmeg. Chill well. Pour into tall mugs or glasses and top generously with beaten egg white slightly sweetened. Insert a sprig of mint into each mug. Spearmint or peppermint will do, but applemint gives it just the right flavor. Serves 8.   South Union

The Shakers were very successful orchardists. At North Union they planted two good-sized orchards at each of their three villages. The same was probably the case throughout Shaker-dom. (It takes seven years for an apple tree to bear fruit.)

In 1840 the yield of fruit at North Union was so great that the year went down in their records as "The Fruitful Year." Six hundred barrels of apples were harvested that season in this small community.

At South Union, in the early 1800's, the Brethren planted 700 apple trees in a single orchard and recorded that "hundreds of peach trees are in full bloom along the creek." On a certain fall day in 1831, 111 barrels of cider were made at their mill. Three days later the Center family put away for its own use 60 barrels of cider, 100 gallons of apple-butter and 1,000 pounds of dried apples.

Certain Shaker beverages were spiced with pepper or ginger, for the Brethren working in the fields in the heat of summer considered them very refreshing. Again, hot ginger tea awaited the ice-cutters on their return home in the winter.

ॐ   ॐ

SHAKER EGGNOG

6 EGGS
4 TABLESPOONS SUGAR
1/2 CUP APPLE BRANDY (IF SERVED TO SICK)
2 QUARTS MILK
1/2 TEASPOON NUTMEG, GRATED

Beat the yolks and whites of eggs separately. Mix sugar with the yolks and add apple brandy, if desired. Mix well while pouring milk very slowly, so it will not curdle. Pour into tall glasses and top with beaten egg white and dust well with nutmeg. This is a very nourishing dish for the sick or aged. It can be served hot. Serves 8.   South Union

ॐ   ॐ

Most of the Shaker communities made excellent fruit wines, cordials and brandy, which were sparingly doled out as prescribed for the aged and sick.

Milk which today is considered the most healthful food, containing almost all the necessary food for bone, nerve and muscle-building, was looked upon with suspicion in the 1700's. The cows which supplied the milk for the cities in those days were kept in dark, filthy pens or stalls within the crowded areas. Often these animals never got outside their stables, never had any exercise or sunlight. They were not fed green food but were given a diet of the fermented grain used to produce alcohol in the nearby distillery. These cattle were often diseased and their milk was watery and extremely poor in nutriment.

By contrast, the Shaker herds presented a wholly different picture. They imported fine cattle. Their barns and stables were models of cleanliness. Often the walls were ceiled and kept spotless. In fair weather the Sisters did the milking. The Shakers had a marked influence on improving dairy conditions in our young land and in furnishing good, wholesome milk to the public. The cattle barns at Hancock and at New Lebanon were model barns in their day.

SHAKER HAYING WATER OR SWITCHEL

4 CUPS SUGAR, OR
   3 CUPS MAPLE SYRUP
2 CUPS MOLASSES
2 TEASPOONS POWDERED GINGER
2 GALLONS COLD WATER

Put all ingredients together and stir until thoroughly blended. Pour into large jug, and chill. Serves 30.

North Union

In haying season, or when the Brethren were working on the roads where they spent double the allotted time in working out the road-tax in order to be exempt from military service, gallons of this thirst-quenching drink, Switchel, was carried to them at regular intervals. Before the Shakers at North Union had ice-houses, they made up gallons of this drink daily during the hot weather, and in order to cool it, they either kept it in their spring-houses or hung the great jugs filled with the beverage down in the wells. Enormous quantities of this drink were consumed each summer by the Brethren working in the shops, fields or when road-building in this part of Ohio.

SHAKER CHOCOLATE

2 OUNCES UNSWEETENED CHOCOLATE

1/2 CUP SUGAR

1 TEASPOON CORNSTARCH

1/8 TEASPOON SALT

2 CUPS BOILING WATER

3 CUPS SCALDED MILK

1 TEASPOON VANILLA

Melt chocolate in saucepan over boiling water (double boiler). Mix cornstarch and salt with sugar and add boiling water; mix thoroughly. Add to melted chocolate and boil for 1 minute. Add scalded, hot milk and heat well while beating mixture with wire whisk. Add vanilla. Serve in warmed cups. Serves 8.   Sister Abigail, North Union

The botanical name for the tree from which chocolate is gathered is called Theobroma, meaning "food of the gods." This enchanting food not only has an irresistible flavor but has high food value as well; starch, fat, protein and many of the chemicals necessary for bone and blood-building are contained therein.

Chocolate was first used in its native land, Mexico, where it was fed in concentrated form to the warriors and long-distance runners, in order to enhance their energy. Long before Columbus set foot on this continent, the Mexicans valued highly their delicious and valuable food. It was the Mexicans who gave it the name 'chocolate.' The ancient artists of that land left us an image of Montezuma quaffing a concoction of chocolate from a golden beaker.

Cortez carried this food to Spain and Portugal, and its use spread rapidly across Europe. It is one of the favorite foods used throughout the world.

38

STRAWBERRY CUP

9 QUARTS STRAWBERRIES

4 CUPS VINEGAR

1 CUP SUGAR TO EACH CUP OF JUICE

Wash, hull and crush the berries. Cover with vinegar and let stand four days. Strain through jelly bag and measure juice. Add sugar and boil gently for 5 minutes. Makes four quarts. Dilute with cold water and serve.

Amelia's Shaker Recipes

ᎨᏕ   ᏸᏱ

SHAKER GRAPE JUICE

2 CUPS GRAPES

1/2 CUP SUGAR

BOILING WATER

Pluck grapes from stem, measure and put in quart jar. Add sugar and fill jar with boiling water and seal. Strain off juice when needed. Serves 4.

Eldress Clymena Miner, North Union

ᎨᏕ   ᏸᏱ

Enormous amounts of this juice were made each fall, for North Union had vast vineyards down below their 1,400-acre farm on the Heights (above Cleveland). Down on the lake shore they owned several hundred acres of well-cultivated vines which spread like a gigantic carpet along the blue waters of Lake Erie. Here the Shakers had a winery where gallons of amber and ruby juice were drained from the ripe clusters each fall. Some of this was converted into medicinal wines and shipped both east and west at market demands. As the Temperance Movement advanced in our land, the demand for unfermented grape juice grew, and the North Union Shakers carried on a thriving business in this commodity. A small Shaker village named Maple Grove was erected near this winery. The daily records and account books of this branch society have never been found and the history of the small community is not widely known.

Breads

Bread-making is one of the most ancient of arts. Archae-ologists have found calcified remains of loaves that date back to the European Stone Age, probably made from a one-grain wheat and barley crushed between stones and mixed with water and subjected to heat. The earliest bread was probably made from acorns. Today the Northwest Pacific Coast Indians still use the acorn in making bread.

In the primitive times, milling and baking were twin arts; the housewife crushed the grain between stones, mixed it with water and shaped it into loaves or cakes which she baked on heated stones or in the ashes. In Biblical times "Lot made a feast and did bake unleavened bread." It is thought, however, that the shew-bread of the Tabernacle was leavened bread as were the barley loaves blessed by Jesus when he fed the multitude in the wilderness.

The ancient Egyptians carried the art of baking to high perfection. White bread made from wheat was used by the rich in that land. Often as many as twenty kinds of bread were served at an Egyptian feast. The commonest kind of loaf among these was round and crusty and resembled our hard roll of today, while other loaves were elongated, sprinkled on top with seed, and greatly resembled our modern Vienna bread.

Greece and Rome also had many kinds of bread. Rome did not establish public bakeries until 168 B.C. The excavations at Pompeii show that some private homes had their own mills and bake-houses in the courtyard, while numerous loaves bearing the stamp of a baker have also been unearthed among the ruins.

In the Middle Ages bakers were subjected to special regulations in all European lands; these laws were supposed to secure fair dealing and protection for the consumer. Bakers were formed into Guilds which were under control of their own officers as well as those of the municipality. In some lands bakers who offended regulations respecting the making and sale of bread were subject to fine, imprisonment and even corporal punishment. In both Turkey and Egypt the bakers who sold light or adulterated bread were nailed by their ears to the doorposts of their shops.

Thus for thousands of years the most widely used food of mankind has been of such overshadowing importance that it has become commonly known as "the staff of life." Although it has differed vastly down through the ages, and even today varies greatly in different parts of the earth, there is, however, general agreement that the principal ingredients are water and some sort of meal or ground cereal. In the most advanced countries wheat is the common grain used, because it makes lighter, better-tasting bread and is more easily digested.

However, as early as 1871 sundry articles appeared in the Shaker *Manifesto,* the official monthly magazine of the Order, on bread. These articles were chiefly protests on the milling of wheat; the millers, it was claimed, were separating and discarding the "live germ of the grain" in their attempt to make flour light in weight and color and subsequently in nourishment. The Shakers went so far as to say in these articles that "what had for countless ages been the staff of life had now become but a weak crutch!"

One of these articles was written by Henry Ward Beecher and is quite modern in thought. He states: "For thousands of years man has eaten without a scientific motive, without rational appreciation of the relation of food to his bones, muscles, nerves and so on. The whole motive of eating lay in the mouth—sheer pleasure to his palate or in the cry of a hungry stomach. Man ate because food tasted good. Before long he ran into dishes which were highly fat-producing. Today we are beginning to see we need muscle-building, nerve-replenishing and bone-building food. ... The host of the future will, instead of asking a guest to take beef pudding and rich desserts, say to a lean, cadaverous visitor, 'Let me fill up your tissues,' or, 'My dear sir, your bones are brittle; therefore allow me to pass you some of this compound'—or, to some exigent scholar, thin and nervous, our host will say, 'My dear fellow, let me help you to some brains; this dish runs strongly to poetry, or is it philosophy you favor? Why, sir, philosophy is only food etherealized!' The day is rapidly approaching when food shall be so nicely adjusted to the human wants and needs that diseases will in a large measure be controlled and the highest physical condition will be attained by the right kinds and amounts of food consumed. . . ."

This article might have sounded a bit exaggerated in its day, but when we now go to our public libraries to draw a cook book, we find ourselves transferred from the fine arts division to the technology department—the once beautiful art of cooking, of making food attractive, savory and appetizing by applying heat and other methods, has become a stark, cold, recognized science where nutritive values, chemical combinations, calories and vitamin content must be dealt with understandingly. Today we learn that what a man eats is so intimately connected with his state of health and well-being that the preparation of foods bears a direct relation to the prosperity and welfare of a people, of a nation and of the world.

The Shakers caught sight of this truth long before domestic science classes were taught in our schools and colleges. They had some definite understanding of the fact that man does not live to eat but eats to live, and consequently they turned to Mother Nature for her fine store of natural foods —fruits, grain, vegetables, greens and herbs—for their necessary sustenance in a day when man lived chiefly upon meats and heavy sweets. Their "cattle upon a thousand hills" furnished them with the milk and milk products that today are considered the complete food. Moreover, they honestly struggled to restore bread to its rightful heritage—the "staff of life"—by insisting that its live germ be retained in milling flour.

SHAKER DAILY LOAF

1/2 CAKE COMPRESSED YEAST
1/8 CUP WARM WATER

1 CUP MILK

1 TABLESPOON BUTTER

1 TABLESPOON SUGAR

1 TEASPOON SALT

3 TO 3 1/2 CUPS SIFTED FLOUR (ALL-PURPOSE)

Dissolve yeast in warm water; scald milk with butter, sugar and salt and stir until well mixed. When lukewarm, add yeast. Gradually add flour until sponge is stiff enough so it does not stick to hands. Place in buttered bowl and brush top with soft butter. Let rise to double its bulk. Knead lightly this time and shape into loaf in pan. Again brush with soft butter and let rise to twice its bulk. Bake in a moderate (350°) oven for 50 minutes. Test loaf by tapping top; if it sounds hollow, the loaf is done. Remove from pan immediately. Cover lightly, for steam must escape. This is an excellent loaf of wholesome, crusty bread. This loaf must not rise very fast or be baked in too hot an oven.

Sister Amelia, North Union

One of the early Shaker bread recipes reads: "Bring in from the spring house a quart of liquid yeast left over from yesterday's baking. Mix with half a cup of salt, a cup of sugar, a cup of butter and enough warm milk to fill a gallon crock. Set near the fire to keep warm while you sift the flour into the dough-tray—a peck and a half of the best wheaten flour. Make a well in the center of the flour and pour in the yeast mixture. Knead until it no longer sticks to your hands. Add flour if necessary. Cover with clean cloth and put lid on dough-tray and shove it near a low fire for the night."

SHAKER WHEATEN BREAD

1 CUP MILK

1 TABLESPOON SALT

4 TABLESPOONS HONEY OR MAPLE SYRUP

3 TABLESPOONS BUTTER

1 CAKE YEAST

1 CUP WARM WATER

2 CUPS WHITE FLOUR, SIFTED

4 CUPS WHOLE WHEAT FLOUR

Scald milk and add salt, sweetening and butter and 3/4 cup warm water and stir well. Let cool to lukewarm. In the remaining 1/4 cup warm water dissolve yeast and add to other liquid mixture. Add flours gradually and knead into a smooth ball. Proceed as with Shaker Daily Loaf (above). Bake in moderate (350°) oven for 50 to 60 minutes. Yields one very substantial loaf of extremely wholesome bread.

Eldress Clymena Miner, North Union

In the olden days the Shakers and others set their sponge in the evening and let it rise all night before the low embers of the open fire. This was the procedure at North Union, when at dawn the kitchen Sisters could be seen lighting fires in the great brick ovens, getting ready for the day's bread-baking. After breakfast huge mounds of dough, which had slowly risen during the night and filled the ample dough-trough, would be taken out and shaped into loaves. The kitchen records show that from twenty to thirty loaves were baked daily back in the days when a hundred Believers gathered thrice daily about the long tables at the center dwelling house. The Shaker brick oven, the outdoor oven and the enormous dough-troughs are things of the past, but good homemade bread fashioned from such recipes as the above will ever remain the "staff of life."

ᑍᐯ   ᑍᐯ

SHAKER BROWN BREAD

1 CUP RYE FLOUR
1 CUP CORNMEAL
1 CUP GRAHAM FLOUR
1 TEASPOON SALT
3/4 TEASPOON SODA
1 3/4 CUPS SOUR MILK
3/4 CUP MOLASSES
2 TABLESPOONS BUTTER, MELTED
1 CUP CHOPPED RAISINS

Sift the dry ingredients together and mix well. Combine in a bowl the sour milk, molasses and melted butter. Combine the two mixtures and stir thoroughly, adding the chopped raisins, lightly floured. Pour into two buttered molds. Fill only two-thirds full. Steam for 2 hours and then bake for 1/2 hour.   Sister Laura, Old Canterbury

ᑍᐯ   ᑍᐯ

"Wheaten loaf freshly taken from the oven should never be eaten while hot no matter how tempting it smells. This rule applies especially to the aged, to children and to those with weak stomachs. All bread should be allowed to 'ripen' before being cut and consumed. Bread goes through a chemical change after baking, when it sends off carbon and other gases while cooling. Always let your bread ripen where it gets plenty of air; do not wrap it or put it into a closed container until it is thoroughly cooled. Never put bread away with any other food, for it absorbs moisture rapidly and takes on foreign flavors."—Sister Laura

47

The original of the above Shaker Brown Bread recipe reads: "To a peck of Indian meal add a peck of Canaille (home-ground wheat with the bran left in). . . . This makes twelve loaves that stick to the ribs."—Old Canterbury Journal

ॐ   ॐ

SISTER ABIGAIL'S SALT RISING BREAD

1 CUP SCALDED MILK

1/2 CUP COARSE CORNMEAL

3 CUPS MILK

3/4 TEASPOON SALT

1 TABLESPOON SUGAR

5 TABLESPOONS LARD OR BUTTER

3 CUPS BREAD FLOUR, SIFTED

2 1/2 CUPS ALL-PURPOSE FLOUR, SIFTED

Scald milk and pour over cornmeal. Let stand in a warm place until bubbles rise to the surface (about 2 1/2 hours). Then heat milk just lukewarm and add to it salt, sugar and shortening and dissolve thoroughly. Now add the corn mixture and set bowl in a dish of lukewarm water until bubbles rise throughout mixture. Then work in sifted bread flour. When well blended, work in sifted all-purpose flour and knead until sponge is very elastic. Divide into three parts and work into loaves. Place in pans and let rise to double the bulk. Place loaves in a moderate (350°) oven for 15 minutes and then increase heat to 425°. Give loaves 1 hour baking in all.   Amelia's Shaker Recipes

ॐ   ॐ

Note that bread flour must be used in the above recipe. Since this is a painstaking recipe, it is best not to reduce the rule to a single loaf. Moreover, the bread gives off such a tempting aroma when baking that one will regret, at this stage, not having doubled the recipe!

Twenty kinds of breads are listed in these early Shaker recipes; among them are Wheaten Loaf, Injun (Indian) Bread, Dyspeptic Loaf, Whey, Rye, Brown, Boston, Rutland Loaf. Many other kinds were named after the perfector of said loaf, such as Sister Lisset's Tea Loaf and Sister Jennie's Potato Bread (see below for recipes for these last two named).

SISTER LISSET'S TEA LOAF

1/2 CAKE YEAST
1 1/2 CUPS MILK
1/4 CUP BUTTER
1 TEASPOON SALT
3 CUPS FLOUR, SIFTED (ABOUT)
2/3 CUP MAPLE SUGAR
1 TEASPOON CINNAMON
1/2 CUP RAISINS
1/2 CUP CURRANTS

Dissolve yeast in a small amount of warm water. Scald milk and add butter and salt. Cool to lukewarm, add yeast and beat in 2 cups of sifted flour. Cover and let stand overnight. In the morning add sugar, cinnamon, raisins and currants and flour enough to work into an elastic ball. Let rise for several hours. Mold into loaf and bake in loaf tin. Let rise until double in bulk and bake in medium (350°) oven for 50 minutes.   Union Village

North Union Household Hints:

"Bread rises more quickly in the day time when the kitchen fires are kept going than at night when only embers smolder on the hearth; therefore four hours in the day time is equal to twelve hours of rising at night. . . . In order to make really good bread, one must have well-milled flour. Use cast-iron bread pans if you want a good crusty loaf. . . . The old brick oven with its even heat baked the best loaf."

"Bread is the one food one can eat thrice daily and not tire of."

"Put all bread crusts and fragments of stale bread in the oven until they are thoroughly dry. Then roll them to a coarse powder with the rolling pin. This crumb is far better in scalloping foods than cracker crumbs which are tasteless and too floury."

"When your cracker barrel has been opened in the summer, the crackers soon lose their crispness. Lay them in a flat pan and heat them slowly in the oven for ten minutes."

SISTER JENNIE'S POTATO BREAD

2 EGGS

1/2 CUP SUGAR

1/4 TEASPOON SALT

1 CUP MASHED POTATOES (UNSEASONED)

1/2 CAKE YEAST

3 CUPS BREAD FLOUR (ABOUT)

1/2 CUP BUTTER

1 CUP WARM WATER

Beat eggs and add 1/4 cup sugar. Add salt and mashed potatoes which have been passed through a sieve. Add yeast which has been dissolved in a little warm water. Stir in enough flour to make a stiff dough. Place in a buttered bread pan and let rise for 2 hours. Then cream butter and the remaining sugar together. Work this into the dough and let rise very slowly for 6 hours. Then work in warm water and shape into loaf. Let rise again until very light, and bake in a quick (450°) oven for 15 minutes; lower heat to 350° and bake until well browned (about 45 minutes).

North Union

SISTER LISSET'S GRAHAM GEMS

Sister Lisset left behind many recipes, among which is one for Graham Gems—which sounds like a tempting Sunday morning dish. Her quaint rule reads: "Stir whatever amount of graham flour your need calls for, into the right proportion of cold water, making a batter that is a trifle thicker than that used for griddle cakes. The secret of success in making tempting gems lies in the mixing; you must stir them rapidly and incorporate as much air into the batter as possible in the four minutes it takes to beat them up. Have your iron gem pans in the oven and have them good and hot and well buttered before pouring the batter. Bake them in a hot oven twenty minutes."

Today this recipe would read:

1 CUP GRAHAM FLOUR
1/2 TEASPOON SALT
1 CUP WATER

Mix and beat four minutes until the bran in the flour has absorbed some of the water. When poured into sizzling buttered gem pans steam will be the leavening agent.

SISTER LOTTIE'S SHAKER GEMS

3/4 CUP BREAD FLOUR, SIFTED
1/4 CUP BRAN
1/2 TEASPOON SALT
1 TEASPOON BAKING POWDER
1 EGG, BEATEN
3/4 CUP WARM MILK
2 TABLESPOONS MOLASSES

Sift the dry ingredients together and add beaten eggs blended with milk and molasses. Beat batter until light and foamy and pour into very hot buttered gem pans. Bake in a quick oven for 15 minutes. These are light and crusty.

Old Canterbury

Union Village Household Hint: "Serve gems on Sabbath morning with plenty of butter and maple syrup." The Shaker communities which made maple syrup usually opened a two-gallon jug of this luscious commodity each Sabbath for breakfast.

From an old Lebanon, New York, Shaker bread recipe we glean: "The first necessary ingredient for wholesome bread is good winter wheat flour. The best bread is made by scalding the white flour thoroughly with very hot milk. It is an art to scald fine white flour. The secret lies in scalding only half the necessary amount of flour and when cool work in the yeast and other necessary ingredients."

Back in the 1830's the millers began bolting the flour (passing it through fine cloth filters). This robbed the flour of much of its vital wheat germ. Both the Shakers and Dr. Sylvester Graham, a food authority of that day, advocated the milling of the entire wheat kernel. This produced "enriched flour"—a term of great significance today.

SISTER HATTIE'S HUCKLEBERRY MUFFINS

2 CUPS FLOUR, SIFTED

1/4 TEASPOON SALT

4 TEASPOONS BAKING POWDER

3 TABLESPOONS SUGAR

1 EGG, BEATEN

1 CUP MILK

2 TABLESPOONS BUTTER, MELTED

1 CUP HUCKLEBERRIES

Sift the dry ingredients together and mix well. Add egg to milk and melted butter and combine with dry ingredients. Dust berries lightly with flour and fold into batter. Drop by spoonsful into well-buttered muffin tins, but do not fill more than one third full, for if the muffins are thin the berries are not so apt to settle to the bottom and the muffins will not be soggy. Bake 25 minutes in a moderate (350°) oven.

Old Watervliet

There is a nostalgic note in the Shaker recipes named after places or towns Down East. Scattered throughout the Household Journals of the various Shaker communities are recipes for Marshfield (Mass.) Cake; Pemigewasset (New Hamp.) Rolls; Rutland (Vermont) Buttermilk Loaf; Chester Muffins and others which must have been hand-copied recipes the good Sisters wrote down before leaving their well-appointed homes on their trek into the Ohio and Kentucky wilderness. Probably many of the recipes came into these parts of our country folded between the covers of Bibles or Hymnals, where many a precious item found safekeeping in the early days!

SHAKER SALLY LUNN

1 CUP MILK

3 TABLESPOONS SUGAR

2 TEASPOONS SALT

1 CUP BUTTER

1 1/2 CAKES YEAST

3 EGGS BEATEN

6 CUPS FLOUR

4 TABLESPOONS BUTTER, FOR BRUSHING

Scald milk. Add sugar, salt, butter and stir until butter melts. Cool to lukewarm and crumble yeast into milk mixture. Stir in the well-beaten eggs. Add flour gradually and beat well. Let rise in a buttered bowl until double its bulk. Knead lightly and place in a Sally Lunn pan (tube cake pan). Brush well with soft butter and bake for 1 hour in medium (350°) oven. Makes a large loaf. Serves 12.   South Union

A North Union dinner menu from the Travel Journal of a visiting Elder, dated July, 1835, reads as follows: "Cold mutton, fresh bread, hoe cakes, fried potatoes, turnip greens, peach preserves, Sally Lunn, tea and milk." The writer of the journal states that the North Union Shakers were serving many meals to the host of Easterners who were migrating west in the 1830's.

Another menu of that same summer mentions "summer soup, lamb stew, baked potatoes, succotash, sliced tomatoes, graham bread, strawberry jam, green apple pie, coffee and milk." This meal must have been served the latter part of August when the first early apples were gathered in! What a treat these early apples offered after months of dried-apple pies or apple-stretched-with-custards or marlboro pies!

In the late 1700's in Bath, England, Sally Lunn sold her

buns and loaves fresh from the oven each morning and evening at a certain street corner. So delicious were they, that
the recipe still bears her name.

ॐ   ܦ

SISTER HARRIET'S COFFEE CAKE

1/2 CAKE YEAST
1 1/4 CUPS WARM WATER
4 CUPS FLOUR
1/4 CUP BUTTER
3 EGGS, BEATEN
1/4 TEASPOON SALT
1/2 CUP SUGAR
2 TABLESPOONS BUTTER, FOR BRUSHING

Dissolve yeast in warm water and add enough flour to
work into a soft ball with your hands. Drop this into a pan
of warm water; cover and let stand in a warm place for an
hour. Then put the remaining flour on a bread board, forming a well in the center and into it put butter, slightly beaten
eggs, salt and sugar. Knead this mass with your hands, gradually working in all the flour. Knead until it becomes a
smooth lump. Now work in the ball of yeast which has been
rising in the bowl of water. Work the whole mass until it is
light and spongy. Now place in a buttered bowl and let rise
until double in bulk. (This should take about 6 hours.)
Knead it again and set in a cold place for 12 hours. Then
work into a flat pan. Let rise for an hour; brush well with
soft butter and sprinkle generously with brown sugar and
cinnamon. Bake about half an hour in 400° oven. This is
well worth the trouble.   North Union

ॐ   ܦ

Sister Harriet Snyder was cook at the guest-house at North Union. She was famous for her original dishes. This toothsome dish may sound like a lot of fuss and bother for a coffee cake, but we must remember that when Sister Harriet fashioned it, she probably multiplied this recipe by six. It is little wonder that some of the visiting Elders recorded in their travel Journals: "We sat down to a most satisfactory supper at North Union, every morsel of which we enjoyed."

SISTER LETTIE'S BUTTERMILK BISCUITS

2 CUPS FLOUR, SIFTED

1/2 TEASPOON SALT

3 LEVEL TEASPOONS BAKING POWDER

1/2 TEASPOON SODA

3 TABLESPOONS BUTTER

3/4 CUP BUTTERMILK

Sift flour, salt, baking powder and soda together. Blend in butter with two knives. Add buttermilk and knead lightly. Roll to 3/4 inch thickness and cut with small cutter. Dab top with melted butter and bake 12 minutes in hot (450°) oven. These are light and delicious. Make plenty!

North Union

North Union Household Hints:

"Do not put the soda into the buttermilk or sour milk as most housewives have been accustomed to do in the past, for this immediately destroys the leavening power of the soda. Treat baking soda as a dry ingredient in baking."

"One cup of heavy sour cream can be substituted in a biscuit recipe for the butter and buttermilk. This recipe makes a splendid shortcake. At North Union we use the buttermilk biscuit recipe for pot pies. Buttermilk makes a far tastier and crustier biscuit than those made with sour milk."

"Chill butter before using in biscuits. This will give you a flakier and more tender hotbread. Do not give your dough when kneading more than eighteen strokes on a lightly floured board."

ह॰   ॰ई

BAKING POWDER BISCUITS

2 CUPS FLOUR, SIFTED
1/2 TEASPOON SALT
3 TEASPOONS BAKING POWDER
1/4 CUP SHORTENING
ABOUT 3/4 CUP MILK

Add salt and baking powder to flour and sift several times. Cut in shortening with pastry blender until thoroughly mixed. Stir in milk to make a soft dough and work lightly on floured board. Roll out to 3/4 inch thickness and cut with standard biscuit cutter. Brush with soft butter and bake in hot (425°) oven from 12 to 15 minutes. Makes 18 biscuits.

ह॰   ॰ई

This same recipe can be used in making drop biscuits; just add 2 extra tablespoons of milk. Stir dough as little as possible and drop by spoonfuls on greased baking sheet. These are called quick or emergency biscuits, for they are very quickly made.

ह॰   ॰ई

CREAM BISCUITS

2 CUPS BREAD FLOUR, SIFTED
3 TEASPOONS BAKING POWDER
1 CUP HEAVY CREAM

Sift flour and baking powder together. Whip cream until stiff; mix lightly with flour, using fork. Turn onto lightly floured board and knead for one minute. Pat dough to 1/2 inch thickness and cut with biscuit cutter. Bake in hot oven (450°) 12 minutes.

Biscuit Hints: If you do not wish to light your oven on a hot day, bake your biscuits on a hot griddle. Grease lightly and place biscuits a good inch apart. Brown on one side for 5 minutes, turn and brown on other side. Very good biscuits! "An almost endless variety of biscuits can be made from any standard recipe by adding grated cheese, minced fruit, berries or spices. No cook is really good without a lively imagination and the will to use it!"—Sister Lisset

Cakes & Cookies

In a hand-written Shaker Household Journal, yellow with age and the buttery fingers of three generations of cooks, we read: "The real skill of a cook is measured by her cake baking; here you can use only the best of butter, eggs and flour, for cakes are so delicate in flavor and depend wholly on the perfect balance and right blending of ingredients— that any shortcoming will soon be detected. . . . Your proportions must be right in cake mixing, therefore it is always wise to use carefully worked out rules and measure all your materials with great exactness. . . . Again, have all your measures, materials and baking tins in readiness, for cake batter must not be left standing after leavening has been added. Above all, see that your oven is at the proper heat for the kind of cake you are perfecting. The matter of proper heat is of utmost importance."

Sugar was very scarce at the western frontier in the early days, and for some years after the founding of our western Shaker communities, maple sugar, maple syrup, molasses and honey were the only sweetenings used, even in cake baking. The oldest cake recipes are all made with the afore-mentioned sweetenings: Molasses Fruit Cake, Maple Sugar Cake, Plumped Raisin Cake, Shaker Wafers (made with boiled molasses) and Shaker Honey Cake. This lack of sugar also accounts for the lack of fluffy, elaborate icings and frostings in the early days.

Later, when granulated sugar was obtainable, there were countless recipes for Sponge, Feather, Marble, Jelly Roll and Pound Cakes, besides hard, soft and old-fashioned Ginger Cake. Then, too, there is an almost endless array of small confections such as crumpets, crullers, sand tarts, sugar cookies, doughnuts, cup cakes, puffs, ginger nuts and jumbles.

MOTHER ANN'S BIRTHDAY CAKE

1 CUP BEST BUTTER

2 CUPS SUGAR

3 CUPS FLOUR, SIFTED

1/2 CUP CORNSTARCH

3 TEASPOONS BAKING POWDER

1 CUP MILK

2 TEASPOONS VANILLA

12 EGG WHITES, BEATEN

1 TEASPOON SALT

Beat butter and sugar into a smooth cream. Sift flour with cornstarch and baking powder. Add flour mixture in small amounts alternately with milk to butter mixture. Beat after each addition, about 200 strokes in all. Add vanilla and lightly fold in the beaten whites of eggs to which the salt has been added. Bake in three layers in a moderate (350°) oven for 25 minutes. When cool fill between layers with peach jelly (see Index), and cover the cake with any delicate icing (see below). This cake is delicious!

Mother Ann's birthday fell on February 29th, but was celebrated on March 1st. The above cake was served at supper, following the long afternoon meeting commemorating the life of the Shakers' beloved founder, Ann Lee (1736-1784). The original recipe reads: "Cut a handful of peach twigs which are filled with sap at this season of the year. Clip the ends and bruise them and beat the cake batter with them. This will impart a delicate peach flavor to the cake."

This same cake was usually baked for the Christmas festival at North Union, when mounds of it were served at the lunch preceding the afternoon meeting. At that season the cake was flavored with rosewater.

In the early days, when granulated or powdered (confectioner's) sugar was very scarce, the North Union Shakers made cake icings by boiling maple syrup and beating it into the stiffly beaten whites of eggs. Later, boiled icings and butter-cream types were used.

SHAKER CAKE ICINGS

Cream Icing
- 2 EGG WHITES
- 3 CUPS POWDERED SUGAR, SIFTED
- PINCH OF SALT
- 1 TEASPOON CREAM
- PEEL OF 1/2 LEMON, GRATED

Beat egg whites very stiff on an open platter; gradually beat in sugar and salt. When mixture stands in peaks, beat in cream and grated lemon peel. Cake must be cold before using this icing.

Boiled Icing
- 1 1/2 CUPS MAPLE OR BROWN SUGAR
- 1/3 CUP WATER
- 2 EGG WHITES
- 1/8 TEASPOON SALT
- 1 TEASPOON VANILLA

Boil sugar and water until it forms a soft ball when tested in cold water. Beat egg whites until very stiff and gradually add hot syrup. Add salt and vanilla and beat until mixture stands in peaks. Spread on warm cake.

Chocolate Icing
- 2 EGG WHITES
- 2 CUPS SUGAR
- 1/4 CAKE CHOCOLATE, GRATED
- 1/2 TEASPOON VANILLA

Beat egg whites until stiff; gradually whip in sugar. Add grated chocolate and vanilla, and beat until smooth.

MAPLE SUGAR CAKE

1 1/2 CUPS MAPLE SUGAR

1/2 CUP BUTTER

2 EGGS, BEATEN

1/2 TEASPOON SALT

1 TEASPOON BAKING SODA

1 TEASPOON CINNAMON

1/2 TEASPOON NUTMEG

2 1/2 CUPS FLOUR, SIFTED

1 1/2 CUPS UNSWEETENED APPLESAUCE

1 CUP RAISINS, CHOPPED

1 CUP HICKORY NUT MEATS

Roll maple sugar until all lumps are crushed. Cream butter, gradually add sugar and beat until creamy. Add beaten eggs and blend thoroughly. Add salt, soda and spices to flour and sift several times. Now alternately add applesauce and dry ingredients to butter mixture and beat well. Lightly flour chopped raisins; combine with nuts and fold into batter. Turn into buttered loaf tin and bake in a moderate (350°) oven for 1 hour.   A very old North Union recipe

SHAKER DRIED APPLE CAKE

1 CUP DRIED APPLES (OR APRICOTS)

1 CUP MOLASSES

2/3 CUP SOUR CREAM

1 CUP SUGAR

1 EGG

1 3/4 CUPS FLOUR, SIFTED

2 TEASPOONS BAKING SODA

1 TEASPOON CINNAMON

1/2 TEASPOON CLOVES

1/2 TEASPOON SALT

Soak dried apples overnight. In the morning cut fine and simmer in molasses for 20 minutes. Cool. Combine cream, sugar and egg and beat until smooth. Combine dry ingredients and sift several times. Blend both mixtures and beat until smooth. Add fruit and molasses. Turn into buttered loaf pan and bake in moderate (350°) oven for 1 hour. This is a very tasty dessert; the dried apples take on a citron flavor.

Union Village

SHAKER THANKSGIVING SPECIALTY

1 CUP BEST BUTTER
4 CUPS SUGAR
7 CUPS FLOUR, SIFTED
8 TEASPOONS BAKING POWDER
1 1/3 CUPS MILK
2 QUARTS HICKORY NUT MEATS, BROKEN
12 EGG WHITES, BEATEN STIFF

Cream butter and sugar. Mix dry ingredients and sift several times, and add alternately with milk to butter mixture. Stir in nut meats, then fold in stiffly beaten egg whites. Turn into 2 buttered tube pans and bake in moderate oven (350°) for 45 minutes. Keep for several weeks to ripen before cutting, for cake improves in flavor if well wrapped and stored.

It was written by one of the North Union Elders that "Every day is Thanksgiving Day at the Shaker communities, for the Believers never cease being thankful for the great bounty God bestows upon His children."

SHAKER CIDER CAKE

1 CUP BUTTER

3 CUPS SUGAR

4 EGGS, BEATEN

1 NUTMEG, GRATED

1/2 TEASPOON SALT

1 TEASPOON SODA

6 CUPS FLOUR, SIFTED

1 CUP CIDER

Cream butter, gradually add sugar and beat thoroughly; then add beaten eggs. Mix all dry ingredients together. Add flour mixture alternately with cider to butter mixture. Butter a loaf pan; turn batter into pan and bake in moderate (350°) oven for 1 hour. When cool, place in tightly closed tin or jar. This cake will keep for weeks.　　　　Union Village

SISTER ABIGAIL'S POUND CAKE

1 CUP BUTTER

1 CUP SUGAR

5 EGGS

1/2 TEASPOON RUM FLAVORING

1/4 TEASPOON MACE

2 CUPS FLOUR, SIFTED

Cream butter thoroughly, and then cream it some more. Gradually work in sugar and beat well. After adding each egg, beat again! Add flavoring and gradually work in the flour. The eggs and the beating furnish the leavening for this cake. Bake for 45 minutes in moderate (350°) oven.

Sister Abigail's Pound Cake was always a delightful baking experience when made in our home many years ago! The careful weighing of exactly 2 pounds of sugar, 2 pounds of butter (which looked like so much good butter for just one cake!). Then the exact weighing of 2 pounds of eggs was the most thrilling part! Often larger or smaller eggs had to be substituted in order to balance the scales in true Shaker fashion. The weighing of the flour was not so exciting, but when the geranium or peach-water extract was uncorked to measure out a scant half teaspoon of one of these exotic flavorings for the great golden mass, life indeed seemed wonderful! The slow baking for three-quarters of an hour perfumed the whole house, and before the great cake was consumed, Sister Abigail had won another star for her crown!

SHAKER GINGER FLUFF

1/2 CUP BUTTER

1/2 CUP SUGAR

2 EGGS, BEATEN

1/2 CUP MOLASSES

2 1/4 CUPS FLOUR, SIFTED

1 1/2 TEASPOONS BAKING SODA

1/2 TEASPOON SALT

1 1/2 TEASPOONS GINGER

1/2 CUP SOUR CREAM

Cream butter and sugar, and fluff well. Add beaten eggs and mix thoroughly. Add molasses. Sift together flour, soda, salt and ginger, putting through sifter several times. Add alternately with sour cream to butter mixture. Pour into buttered tin and bake in moderate (350°) oven for 45 minutes. Serve very hot with Lemon Sauce (see below). Serves 8 generously.

Eldress Clymena Miner, North Union

Ginger, made from the hot and pungent root of the Zinzibar plant, has for centuries been widely used in cookery and medicine. In ancient Germany and England cakes of fanciful forms, and flavored with ginger and often gilded, were given as gifts to children at festivals. These undoubtedly were the ancestors of our gingerbread boy. Ginger is given in the standard dictionary as a verb, meaning to make lively, to animate.

LEMON SAUCE

1/2 CUP SUGAR

1/2 CUP BUTTER

1 EGG, BEATEN

1 TEASPOON LEMON RIND, GRATED

1/2 CUP BOILING WATER

JUICE OF 1 LEMON

DASH OF NUTMEG

Cream sugar and butter together. Add egg and grated lemon rind. Set in pan of boiling water; gradually add boiling water to sauce, stirring constantly. Heat over water for 5 minutes. Add lemon juice and nutmeg. Serve hot.

SHAKER FOAMY SAUCE

1/2 CUP WATER

1 CUP SUGAR

2 EGG YOLKS

1/2 TEASPOON SALT

2 TEASPOONS VANILLA

1 CUP WHIPPED CREAM

Boil water and sugar together until it forms a soft ball when tested in cold water. Beat egg yolks and salt together. Add vanilla and pour syrup over; beat all together until cool. Fold in whipped cream. Very good on any pudding.

SISTER LETTIE'S CRULLERS

1/4 CUP BUTTER

1 CUP SUGAR

3 EGGS, BEATEN

1 TEASPOON SALT

1 TEASPOON BAKING POWDER

1/2 TEASPOON NUTMEG

ABOUT 3 1/2 CUPS BREAD FLOUR, SIFTED

1/3 CUP MILK

Cream together butter and sugar and add beaten eggs. Sift salt, baking powder, nutmeg and flour together several times and add alternately with milk to butter mixture. Form dough into soft ball and let stand 2 hours. Roll out to 1/2 inch thickness and cut into diamond shapes with pastry wheel. Make an inch slash at center, which is aid in frying. Drop into boiling fat and fry to golden brown. Sprinkle while hot with powdered sugar. Are delicious served hot. Makes about 3 dozen.

Doughnuts, fried cakes and crullers originated centuries ago on "Fetter Dienstag" (Fat Tuesday), Shrove Tuesday, which was a day of festival and fun at the very beginning of the long Lenten season of penances. It was on this day that the people were supposed to use up the "fat, flesh and eggs which in olden times were forbidden during the forty days of Lent," in most European lands. A sweetened raised dough was made and the entire family participated in shaping these "nuts and nuggets" of dough and frying them in deep fat. These were eaten throughout the day.

There are many delightful legends concerning the origin of the hole in the doughnut. Most authorities grant to the medieval Dutch housewife the credit for removing the often soggy, unbaked center from this popular confection; it is now done before frying, thus eliminating any chances of culinary failure in making "fat cakes" or doughnuts.

SHAKER SUGAR COOKIES

1 CUP BEST BUTTER
2 CUPS SUGAR
3 EGGS
1/2 TEASPOON LEMON PEEL, GRATED
1/4 TEASPOON NUTMEG
3/4 TEASPOON CREAM OF TARTAR
1 TEASPOON SALT
4 TO 4 1/2 CUPS FLOUR, SIFTED

Cream butter and sugar. Save 1/2 egg white for brushing cookies. Slightly beat the remaining eggs and add to butter mixture. Add grated lemon peel and nutmeg. Sift cream of tartar and salt with flour and work into butter mixture.

Form into ball, cover and chill for half an hour. Roll out to 1/2 inch thickness and cut with large round cookie cutter. Brush with egg white and sprinkle generously with sugar. Bake in hot (400°) oven for 10 minutes. Makes about 3 dozen cookies.   Eldress Clymena Miner, North Union

The great cookie crock at North Union was usually filled with these cookies, for these good Shakers had butter and eggs aplenty in those days. Many an early settler in those parts who knew the Shakers fondly retains the delightful taste memory of these simple but delicious Sugar Cookies.

If you wish a very crisp, brittle ginger cookie, try this Shaker recipe.

SHAKER GINGER CHIPS

1 CUP MOLASSES
1/4 CUP BUTTER
1 TEASPOON GINGER
1 TEASPOON SODA
1/4 TEASPOON SALT
1/2 TEASPOON BAKING POWDER
2 1/4 CUPS FLOUR, SIFTED

Bring molasses to a full boil; add butter and stir well. Remove from fire. Sift dry ingredients together and work into the hot mixture. Chill well. When cold, roll very thin and cut out with large round cutter. Bake in hot (400°) oven. Watch carefully, for these ginger chips burn easily; in fact, anything containing molasses does.

SISTER LETTIE'S SAND CAKES

1 CUP BUTTER

2 CUPS SUGAR

1 TEASPOON LEMON RIND, GRATED

3 EGG WHITES

3 1/2 CUPS FLOUR, SIFTED

1 TEASPOON SALT

1 TEASPOON BAKING POWDER

1/2 CUP NUTS, BLANCHED AND CHOPPED

Cream butter and sugar together; add grated lemon rind and egg whites and mix well. Sift flour, salt and baking powder together. Blend with butter mixture and chill well. Then roll very thin and sprinkle with chopped nuts. Cut with pastry wheels into small squares. Place on cooky sheet and bake in moderate (350°) oven for 8 minutes; dust while hot with sugar and cinnamon and return to oven for 2 minutes. This is a very ancient, favored recipe. You will be well rewarded for your labor in making them. These keep if hidden away. Makes about 5 dozen small cakes.

Sand tarts or cakes were long, long ago known as "Saints' Hearts" and had their origin in the early Christian Church when on saints' days small cakes were baked in the shape of hearts; they were also called Life Cakes. In the museum at Bath, England, there is a collection of cutters used in making these cakes. Later these cakes were ornamented and given as gifts on saints' days. The name, strangely, became distorted from Saints' Hearts to Sand Tarts. This ancient recipe found its way into the Shaker kitchens and became a favorite among them, perhaps because like the Shaker food these little sand tarts were once upon a time tinctured with religious zeal.

SHAKER SOUR CREAM COOKIES

1 CUP SUGAR

3 EGGS, BEATEN

1 CUP SOUR CREAM

3/4 TEASPOON SODA

1/4 TEASPOON NUTMEG

3 CUPS FLOUR

Cream sugar and beaten eggs, and add cream. Mix dry ingredients and add to egg mixture. Drop by spoonfuls on buttered and floured cooky sheet. Bake in hot (400°) oven. These are wonderfully good. This is an old recipe from the Enfield community.   Sister Marguerite, Canterbury

SHAKER SEED CAKES

1/2 CUP BUTTER

1 1/2 CUPS SUGAR

3 EGGS

1 TEASPOON ANISE SEED

3 CUPS FLOUR

1/2 CUP ALMONDS, BLANCHED

Use only the best butter and cream well. Add sugar gradually and beat. Add one egg at a time and beat after each is added. Mix in the anise seed and gradually work in the flour. Roll to 1/2 inch thickness. Place on lightly buttered cookie sheet and cut into diamond shapes (1 1/2 inches long) with pastry wheel. Brush with egg white and press whole blanched almond into center of each diamond. Bake in a moderate (350°) oven.

The recipe for these, penned into my mother's old manuscript cook book, adds this bit of advice: "Let these cakes ripen for several days before serving. Keep in an earthen jar, well out of sight, for they are very tempting!"

Corn Dishes

It is impossible even to touch upon the subject of Shaker cookery without paying due respect to corn—the food which played such an important role in the settlement of this great land. The United States Department of Agriculture bulletin of April, 1934, on "The American Indian's Contribution to Civilization," states: "For several years after their foundation the first colonists faced starvation, and they survived not only because they received supplies from the mother country but chiefly because they made purchases and thefts of corn from the Indians. The permanence of the colonies was assured only when they were established agriculturally, and this came when they had adopted the crops and tillage methods of the Indians. Governor Bradford, referring to Squanto (an English-speaking Indian) tells how he came to the relief of the Pilgrim Fathers, 'Showing them both ye manner how to set corn and how to dress and tend it. Also, he told them except they got small fish and set them with the seeds [as fertilizers] it should come to nought.' "

This meant that the ground was cleared and exposed to the sunlight by girdling the trees or by scotching the roots. Later the trunks and stumps were burned. This Indian method of clearing the land was practiced clear across the nation by many of the pioneers. History tells us that the Spaniards who followed Coronado, the French who sailed with Champlain, the Virginians under Sir Walter Raleigh, the Puritans under Brewster, the Quakers under Penn, the Swedes settling along the Delaware and the Dutch along the Hudson, "All found in the Redman's maize [corn] a food which sustained them and was vital to their existence while they conquered those who gave it to them to eat. The white man rose up refreshed and built cities of the New World on the cornfields of the Indian."

In the early annals of the Shaker communities we find this history repeated. Corn was the staple food at the frontier. In the newly turned sod the European grains, such as wheat, barley and rye, were slow in getting started; corn alone yielded a fair harvest. Especially in Ohio, Kentucky and Indiana Shaker communities, these pioneers worked from dawn to dark to eke out a scant existence. With the many strangers within their gates, with constant visitations from their spiritual leaders Down East, the food problem was a tremendous one! In MacLean's *Shakers of Ohio* we read: "At first [early 1800's] it was Lent with them most of the time. Meat with them, as in all pioneer localities, was very scarce and most of the time they were without milk for their large families. Bread was also generally lacking; Indian bread and corn was their chief diet." When sweet corn was in season, these early western Shakers ate roasting ears thrice daily. This was supplemented with corn dishes such as their forefathers had learned to concoct from the Indians—suppone (pone), samp (corn mush), hominy, succotash and Indian pudding.

We might say it was the Indian squaw who conducted the first domestic science classes in America, for it was she who planted and harvested the Indian maize and it was she who treated its firm, hard kernels with lye and pounded them in mortars into meal and flour. Again, it was she who shaped this precious substance into loaves and cakes and baked them before an open fire or encased them in leaves and buried them in hot ashes. It was from the Indian squaw that we learned to mix cornmeal with water and bake it into pone. In her earthen pot she added meal to boiling water and made samp or porridge. For variety's sake she added fat, crushed fruit and maple syrup to her cornmeal and fashioned an Indian pudding, and she roasted and boiled green corn in season. In her pot she added beans to her whole-kernel corn and made succulent succotash. She discovered the well-known dish—hominy; she parched corn, she popped it and she made many tasty dishes by adding berries, meat and wild honey. All these our early forefathers borrowed from the squaw. More than 300 years have ripened the old recipes; we have added eggs and other substances and the flavors have mellowed with time; chemists and dietitians have brought about improvements, but the old rules still retain some of their flavor and remind us of the debt America owes the Redman.

Corn was the staple diet among the western Shakers in the early days and for the many years which followed; they ate it, they stuffed their ticks with its husks; they made braided rugs for their thresholds; they fed it to their cattle, and used it as fodder for the hogs; they made of the cobs pipes for their old men and toys for their children. The dried cobs also furnished them with fuel.

"The Valleys shall stand full of corn; they shall laugh and sing." Psalm 65.

ॐ   ॐ

SHAKER JOHNNY CAKE

2 CUPS CORNMEAL

1/2 TEASPOON SALT

1 TEASPOON BAKING SODA

1 CUP SOUR MILK

1/2 CUP MOLASSES

1 CUP SUET, FINELY CHOPPED

Sift cornmeal, salt and soda together several times until well blended. Add sour milk and molasses and fold in chopped suet. Bake in a shallow pan 30 minutes at 400°. Serves 6.

Whitewater

ॐ   ॐ

One of the old recipes for Johnny Cake reads: "Mix the cornmeal with milk or water and form with your hands into small cakes and bake on a board before an open fire." This made a very hard cake, for it was made without shortening and without leavening. It was this hard crust which enabled our pioneer forefathers to carry it with them as their chief sustenance on long journeys, whence it derived its name Journey Cake which was later contracted to Johnny Cake. On consumption it had to be dipped into cider or water in order to soften the hard crust.

Before the Shaker grist mills were grinding, the Shakers used stump-mortars in preparing their meal. It took two hours to grind enough corn by this method to supply enough meal for one person for a day. Imagine the task of grinding enough for the entire North Union community!

When the early Shaker Brethren were building roads or working in distant fields, they sometimes took cornmeal with them which they mixed with water and shaped into small cakes and baked on their hoes over an open fire; hence the name hoecake. When they acquired herds and raised poultry, these primitive recipes had milk, eggs and shortening added to them, and developed into the delicious dishes that we enjoy today.

SISTER SALLIE'S SOUR CREAM CORN BREAD

1 CUP YELLOW CORNMEAL

1 CUP WHEAT FLOUR

1 TEASPOON SALT

2 TABLESPOONS SUGAR

1 TEASPOON BAKING SODA

1 TEASPOON CREAM OF TARTAR

1 CUP LIGHT SOUR CREAM

4 TABLESPOONS MILK

1 EGG

1 TABLESPOON SOFT BUTTER

Blend cornmeal, flour, salt, sugar, soda and cream of tartar and run through a horsehair sieve several times until well mixed. Now add the cream, milk, egg, slightly beaten and the soft butter and stir thoroughly. Turn into a shallow buttered pan and bake 20 minutes in a fairly hot (425°) oven. This makes a light, delicious corn bread. Serves 6.

Whitewater

In 1854 an article appeared in an eastern science journal on the too extensive use of soda (bicarbonate of soda) in this country. It was claimed that the average annual intake per person at that time amounted to several pounds: it was widely used in boiling vegetables, in sweetening drinks, in baking, and in neutralizing acid in pieplant, cranberries and other tart foods. The physician who wrote the article claimed (as all physicians know today) that the use of large amounts of soda was dangerous to health, especially that of children. He went so far as to state that the high child mortality of that day was largely because of this overdosage of soda, which left the stomach too alkaline, causing digestive disturbances.

The Shakers read these science journals at their weekly social meetings and discussed them. This particular article, it is said, brought about a decided decrease in the use of soda among them. Recipes using baking powder soon displaced the delicious "sodie biscuit."

SHAKER HOMINY CAKES

2 CUPS HOMINY

2 EGGS, BEATEN

1 TEASPOON SALT

1 TEASPOON SUGAR

1 CUP WHEAT FLOUR

2 CUPS MILK

Cook the hominy in salted water until tender. Pour off water and cool. Add beaten eggs, salt, sugar, flour and milk. Drop with small ladle on hot buttered griddle. Brown on both sides to a rich golden color and serve with dinner in place of vegetable, or serve for breakfast. The bit of sugar will help brown the cakes. Makes 15 cakes.

ह৹   ৽ई

The Shakers made large quantities of hominy in the early days. This was a lengthy procedure, for the corn had to be soaked in lye water overnight after it was shelled. The following morning it was boiled in the water in which it had been soaked. This boiling process lasted three hours. The corn was then washed and rubbed until the hulls came off, when it was again boiled and drained, and boiled and drained for yet a third time. A teaspoon of salt per quart of water was added to the last boiling.

Hominy is made from white corn; "hulled corn" is made from yellow corn.

Among the "Shaker Corn Recipes" are found recipes for making corn puddings, fritters, oysters, relishes, chowders, puffets, muffins and sundry other toothsome and delicious dishes such as succotash, hog'n'hominy, grits, pig's head cheese and both baked and boiled puddings.

ह৹   ৽ई

SHAKER SCRAPPLE

2 CUPS PORK, COOKED AND GROUND

3 QUARTS OF BROTH FROM COOKED MEAT

1 1/2 TEASPOONS SALT

1/8 TEASPOON SAGE

1/8 TEASPOON MARJORAM

1/2 TEASPOON PEPPER

2 CUPS CORNMEAL

2 CUPS WHOLE WHEAT FLOUR

Boil pork in 4 quarts of water; drain (keeping 3 quarts

liquid). Chop meat fine. Bring broth to boil and add seasoning. Mix cornmeal and whole wheat flour and stir into boiling mixture along with the chopped meat. Cook slowly in
a heavy pot for 30 minutes, stirring frequently. Pour into
dishes or loaf pans. When cold, slice 1/4 inch thick and fry
in hot fat until well browned on both sides.   North Union

The original recipe for this wholesome dish reads: "Take
the hog jowls, the feet, part of the liver and the tongue.
Cleanse thoroughly and put into a large pot to boil. Cook
until the meat falls from the bones. Salvage broth. Chop the
meat fine. Season the broth (10 quarts) with salt, sage,
marjoram (do not be stingy with marjoram) and pepper.
Place over fire and when it boils add chopped meat and
cornmeal and wheaten flour mixed in equal parts. (Buckwheat flour was often used.) Cook slowly for a half hour and
stir frequently. Dish out into loaf pans. When cold slice
down in 1/4 inch slices and fry to a golden brown as you
would mush. This is a very nice breakfast dish."

Scrapple had a definite season. It started with the first
fall frost and lasted until the return of warm weather the
following spring. Due to the fat content of the pork, scrapple
did not keep in the warm weather. This dish was an excellent
way of using up pork scraps when butchering: its name
probably originated thus. It is a Pennsylvania Dutch dish,
and may have come into the Shaker cookery collection
through the small and short-lived Philadelphia Shaker
Society.

GREEN CORN SOUFFLÉ

2 TABLESPOONS BUTTER

2 TABLESPOONS FLOUR

1 CUP MILK

1/2 TEASPOON SALT

1 TABLESPOON SUGAR

1/8 TEASPOON PEPPER

3 EGGS

2 CUPS GREEN CORN, GRATED

Make a white sauce by melting butter and adding flour, then blending well over a low heat. Gradually add the milk and stir until smooth. Add salt, sugar and pepper. Beat the yolks and whites of eggs separately. Add the beaten yolks to the white sauce and mix thoroughly. Add corn and let cool slightly. Now fold in the stiffly beaten whites. Pour into a buttered baking dish and bake 45 minutes in a moderate (325°) oven. Serve at once. Serves 6.　　　　North Union

"A soufflé must never be kept waiting!"—Sister Lisset.

A good rule for boiling roasting ears: "Always cook roasting ears as soon as possible after pulling. Remove the outer husks but leave on the inner layer. Fold back and remove every fibre of corn silk. Place the ears in a kettle with just enough cold water to cover; add a tablespoon of sugar and let come to a boil. Allow it to boil just one minute. By no means add salt while boiling, for this toughens the corn and draws out the sugar. Serve immediately with plenty of butter, salt and pepper."

This is an excellent recipe and has been used for years in the home of the writer, who varies the rule by removing all the husk before boiling, placing a handful of sweet inner husks in the bottom of the kettle. This greatly enhances the flavor of the corn, and is far simpler than removing the husks from the very hot ear.

GREEN CORN PUDDING

2 CUPS GRATED GREEN CORN
3 EGGS
1/4 CUP SUGAR
DASH OF NUTMEG
1/2 TEASPOON SALT
1/8 TEASPOON PEPPER
2 CUPS RICH MILK
1/2 CUP BREAD CRUMBS, BUTTERED
2 TABLESPOONS BUTTER

Grate uncooked kernels from fresh corn. Put in buttered baking dish. Beat eggs well; add sugar, nutmeg, salt, pepper and milk, and blend. Sprinkle top with buttered bread crumbs and dot with butter. Place in a dish of boiling water and bake in slow (250°) oven for 1 hour. Serves 6.

Amelia's Shaker Recipes

In the early North Union annals we read: "Corn was our most valued single article of food. It not only fed our members in the early days, but also our cattle and hogs. In season we ate it from the cob thrice daily. What was left we cut from the cob and dried for winter use. In the early days we dried it on sheets in the sun but in later years we had a drying house where small wood-burning stoves furnished a gentle heat. We dried hundreds of pounds of corn in this fashion every year. Whatever was not consumed by our large household was sold in the neighboring markets by our peddler."

At one time drying sweet corn was the chief industry of the Sisters at North Union.

ह‍‍े०   ५‍‍े

INDIAN GRIDDLE CAKES

1 CUP CORNMEAL

1 CUP WHITE FLOUR

1/2 TEASPOON SALT

1 TEASPOON BAKING POWDER

1/2 TEASPOON BAKING SODA

2 EGGS

2 TABLESPOONS MELTED BUTTER

2 CUPS BUTTERMILK

Sift cornmeal, flour, salt, baking powder and soda together. Add slightly beaten egg yolks and melted butter to buttermilk and beat the two mixtures together. Fold in the stiffly beaten egg whites. Bake on a hot griddle. A soapstone griddle greased with a ham rind makes the tastiest griddle cakes. Fry to a rich brown. Cornmeal requires longer frying than wheaten cakes. Makes 8 generous cakes.   Watervliet, Ohio

ह‍‍े०   ५‍‍े

An excellent spread for griddle cakes is made with 2 cups of maple syrup which has boiled for 5 minutes, to which 2 tablespoons of the best butter are added. Remove from fire, stir smooth and serve very hot.

ह‍‍े०   ५‍‍े

CORN OYSTERS

2 EGG YOLKS
2 CUPS FRESH CORN, GRATED
1/2 TEASPOON SALT
1/4 TEASPOON PEPPER
1/4 CUP FLOUR
3 EGG WHITES, STIFFLY BEATEN

Add the beaten egg yolks to the grated corn and add salt and pepper. Mix in flour and fold in the well-beaten egg whites. Drop onto a well-greased skillet in globs the size of an oyster. Brown on both sides and serve at once. Makes 12. A very nice side dish with cold meat.

Desserts

What never-to-be-forgotten fragrances would have whetted our appetites if we could have visited the mammoth Shaker kitchens when a dozen pungent puddings aquiver with lush spices, dark juicy molasses and hours and hours of slow baking in the old brick ovens emerged at dinner time! Often this fragrance was mingled with that of rows and rows of steaming berry pies or small hills of doughnuts still wreathed in the aroma of hot butter and nutmeg!

There are several references made in the Travel Journals of Shakers visiting at North Union when, in honor of their guests, the Shakers served picnic suppers in their far-famed Hemlock Grove. On these occasions there emerged from their great food hampers substantial dishes such as baked hash, "Shaker fish and eggs," scalloped potatoes, huge loaves of freshly baked bread to be sliced on the spot and spread with tasty herb-butters; and there were crocks of crisp pickles and a whole array of juicy pies and slabs of cake as well as crullers, tarts and quantities of fresh cold milk.

In Mary Whitcher's *Shaker Housekeeper* we read recipes for Spanish Creams, Chocolate Pudding, Steamed Puddings with various sauces, Snow Pudding with a Golden Sauce; Baked Cornstarch, Apple, Bread and Butter, Rice, Sago and Plum Puddings; recipes for Ambrosia and nineteen varieties of cakes and an equal assortment of cookies; for Creams, Gelatines, Baked Fruits, Pan Dowdy and countless cranberry dishes, for Soufflés and Custards besides Pies, Dumplings and Tarts.

We read: "Food was good at the Shaker communities and the lusty appetites of the hard workers of their households, and of their many guests who often had traveled many miles, complimented the Shaker cooks."

SHAKER APPLE DUMPLINGS

4 TART APPLES
PASTRY FOR TWO 9-INCH CRUSTS (SEE INDEX)
1/2 CUP SUGAR
2 TABLESPOONS CREAM
1 TABLESPOON ROSEWATER (SEE INDEX)
1/2 CUP HOT MAPLE SYRUP

Select large, pleasantly sour apples. Peel and core apples.

86

Roll pastry thin and cut into squares large enough to wrap around apple. Place apple in middle of pastry square; fill center of apple with well-blended mixture of sugar, cream and rosewater. Bring corners of pastry square together and wet edges so they will cling together when pressed about apple. Prick pastry with fork. Place in baking dish and bake 15 minutes in hot (450°) oven. Baste with hot syrup and reduce heat to 350°; bake another 30 minutes. Baste with syrup every 15 minutes. Serve with Hard Sauce (see below). Serves 4.   Amelia's Shaker Recipes

There were very few flavoring extracts in the early days. Almost every household made its supply of rosewater which was used to flavor pies, cakes, puddings and custards. Grated orange and lemon peel were also used for this purpose. The Shakers made great quantities of rosewater. This extract has a very subtle and delightful flavor. It will furnish a new and happy gustatory thrill when tried. (See Index for Shaker recipe.)

HARD SAUCE

1/3 CUP BUTTER
1 CUP SUGAR, POWDERED, MAPLE OR BROWN

Cream butter and gradually work in sugar. Form into balls or squeeze through paper cone into fancy shapes; dust with nutmeg. Chill before serving. When added to warm dumplings or puddings, the sauce melts down slowly and mingles its delicate flavor with that of the dessert.

STRAWBERRY SHORT CAKE

1 TEASPOON SALT
2 TABLESPOONS SUGAR
2 TEASPOONS BAKING POWDER
2 CUPS FLOUR, SIFTED
4 TABLESPOONS BUTTER
2/3 CUP LIGHT CREAM
SOFT BUTTER
2 QUARTS RIPE BERRIES
1/2 CUP SUGAR

Add salt, sugar and baking powder to flour and sift several times. Work in the butter with a pastry blender; add cream. Handle dough as little as possible. Divide into two equal parts and roll out each to 3/4 inch thickness. Spread with soft butter and place one on top of the other. Bake in a hot (450°) oven about 12 minutes. Split apart; fill with a deep layer of berries which have been hulled and crushed and to which sugar is added. Put on top crust and cover with remaining berries. Serve with thick cream. Serves 6-8.

Eldress Clymena Miner, North Union

STRAWBERRY SAUCE

1 EGG WHITE
1 CUP STRAWBERRIES, WELL MASHED
1 CUP POWDERED SUGAR
2 TABLESPOONS SOFT BUTTER

Beat egg white very stiff; fold in crushed berries and beat until light and fluffy. Then gradually add sugar and beat until mixture stands in peaks. Then add soft butter and keep on beating. It is best to make this on an open platter so that plenty of air is beaten into the sauce. This can be used as a topping for shortcake or can be used as a sauce for a plain cake, turning it into a delightful desert. Old recipe.

Sister Lottie, Canterbury

BUSY-DAY DESSERT

1 CUP WATER

6 LARGE TART APPLES

1 CUP SOUR CREAM

3/4 TEASPOON SODA

3 TABLESPOONS SUGAR

1/4 TEASPOON NUTMEG

1 RECIPE DROP BISCUITS (SEE INDEX, BAKING
  POWDER BISCUITS)

Set your pot on the stove. Put in 1 cup of water; add six large tart apples which have been peeled and quartered. To a cup of cream add soda, sugar and nutmeg and pour over apples. Top with drop biscuit dough, cover tightly and bake in medium (325°) oven for 1 hour.

PUDDING IN HASTE

1/2 CUP SUET, FINELY CHOPPED

2 CUPS STALE BREAD CRUMBS

1 CUP CURRANTS

1/2 TEASPOON GINGER

GRATED PEEL OF 1 LEMON

6 EGG YOLKS PLUS 2 WHITES

1/2 CUP SUGAR

1 CUP FLOUR

When company arrives unexpectedly, this is a good dish to

make quickly. Chop suet fine and add bread crumbs. Then add currants, ginger and lemon peel. Beat egg yolks and whites and sugar together and add to mixture. Blend well and shape into balls the size of a goose egg. Roll in flour and drop into boiling pot. Twenty minutes will see them rising to the top when they are done. Serve very hot with wine or cider sauce. Serves 8.   South Union

On Making Puddings: "The outside of some boiled puddings taste disagreeable—sort of musty. This is due to the pudding cloth not being kept for puddings only! Or perhaps the cloth has not been boiled out or washed properly after each using. . . . Each time before using, your pudding cloth should be dipped in boiling water, squeezed out dry and well dusted with flour. If bread crumbs are used in the pudding, the bag must be tied loosely; if batter is used, tie bag very tightly. The pudding pot must be boiling very hard when the pudding is plunged in. Have a pot of cold water in readiness to dip boiling pudding into immediately as it comes from the boiling, otherwise it will adhere to cloth."—Sister Lettie

AMELIA'S QUINCE PUDDING

6 LARGE QUINCES
1 CUP SUGAR
1 CUP HEAVY CREAM
1/4 CUP ROSEWATER (SEE INDEX)
6 EGG YOLKS, BEATEN
6 EGG WHITES, BEATEN STIFF

Rub fuzz from 6 large ripe quinces; pare and quarter them (save the peels for jelly and the seeds for quincewater).

Grate quinces to a pulp; add sugar and cream and mix well. Add rosewater and beaten yolks of eggs. Fold in the stiffly beaten egg whites. Turn into a well-buttered baking dish and bake 45 minutes at 350°. Serves 4.   North Union

ह॰   ॰ई

Shaker desserts were usually prepared for eight persons, for the serving at table was done in units of eight. Young Sisters were assigned to this task. Amelia's Quince Pudding, as given above, is just half the original recipe. For a full-sized Shaker family of one hundred persons, twenty-four such recipes were prepared for a single dinner.

ह॰   ॰ई

PUDDING SAUCE

1 CUP SUGAR
2 TABLESPOONS CORNSTARCH
PINCH OF SALT
2 CUPS BOILING WATER
2 TABLESPOONS BUTTER
JUICE OF 1 LEMON

Mix sugar, cornstarch and salt in saucepan and add boiling water. Mix well; add butter and cook 5 minutes. Add lemon juice. Serve very hot. Most any flavoring can be added to this basic recipe; try adding 2 tablespoons of rosewater, or a glass of grape jelly, or 2 tablespoons of any fruit cordial, or a half cup of boiled-down cider.

ह॰   ॰ई

Perhaps the origin of the word dessert meant to the Shakers just what it implies, a reward or a just dessert for "Shakering their plate," which means they never helped themselves to more food than they wanted and ate all they took!

91

SHAKER INDIAN PUDDING

3/4 CUP CORNMEAL

1 CUP DARK MOLASSES

1 TEASPOON SALT

4 CUPS HOT MILK

1/4 TEASPOON GINGER

1/4 TEASPOON NUTMEG

1 TABLESPOON BUTTER

2 CUPS COLD MILK

Butter your bean pot well. Put in cornmeal, molasses and salt; add the scalded milk and let set overnight. The next morning add ginger, nutmeg, butter and a cup of the cold milk and stir well. Bake in a very slow oven until a crust forms on top. Stir thoroughly and add the other cup of cold milk. Bake slowly for 4 more hours in a very slow oven. Stir several times while baking. When a good crust has formed, cover the pot. Serve with cream or hard sauce. Serves 6.

Union Village

The original recipe for this famous old dish dates back to the days when the Shaker Sisters still used the old brick ovens. The directions read: "Bake from eight in the morning till four in the afternoon. This is a very tasty and favorite dish."

Appone was a favorite dessert dish among the Western Reserve pioneers and consequently was often served at North Union. It was an Indian dish consisting of cornmeal, maple syrup and crushed fruit (usually wild), or berries, and baked slowly in a pot. It was usually served with butter.

Earliest Shaker baking rules: "Bake your cake until it is golden brown and has shrunk away from the sides of the pan. . . . Bake your custards until they plump up in the middle."

The Compleat Housewife, an English cook book of 1683 states: "The Housewife should be cleanly both of body and garments; she must have a quick eye, a curious nose, a perfect taste, and a most ready ear to catch the first boil. . . ."

CHRISTMAS BREAD PUDDING

Butter an ample baking dish. Cover the bottom with fairly thick slices of bread generously buttered. Then add a goodly layer of currants, also one of shredded citron, of candied orange peel and candied lemon peel, if you have it. Then spread with a layer of strawberry jam, not too thin, for remember it is Christmas! Then repeat these layers until the dish is two-thirds filled. Then pour over this an unboiled custard made of plenty of eggs and rich milk; remember it is Christmas! Let stand for at least two hours. Then add a pretty fluting of your best pastry around the very edge of the dish; this touch is not necessary but it adds much to the gayety of the dish. Now bake until the crust is well set and the top is a rich and appetizing golden brown. Eat it with much relish, for remember it is Christmas!

EXCELLENT PUDDING SAUCE

2 CUPS BROWN OR MAPLE SUGAR

2 TABLESPOONS CORNSTARCH

1/2 TEASPOON SALT

2 CUPS BOILING WATER

2 TABLESPOONS BUTTER

2 TABLESPOONS VINEGAR

1 TEASPOON VANILLA

1/8 TEASPOON NUTMEG

Mix sugar, cornstarch and salt; add boiling water and boil for 5 minutes, stirring frequently. Then add butter, vinegar, vanilla and nutmeg, and blend. Serve very hot.

SHAKER CHRISTMAS PUDDING

2 POUNDS RAISINS

1/2 PINT WINE OR CIDER FOR PLUMPING RAISINS

1 POUND SUET, CHOPPED FINE

12 EGGS, SEPARATED

1 PINT MILK

1/2 CUP MAPLE SYRUP

2 QUARTS FLOUR

1 1/2 TEASPOONS SALT

1 TEASPOON MACE

1 TABLESPOON CINNAMON

1 TABLESPOON GINGER

Plump raisins overnight in wine or boiled cider. Drain well but keep liquid. Cream chopped suet. Add beaten egg yolks to milk and maple syrup. Mix dry ingredients and combine all except egg whites, even the wine or cider in which the raisins were plumped. Beat egg whites and fold into mixture. Pour into a strong pudding bag which has been wet and well dusted with flour. Do not tie too tightly, for remember the pudding will swell. Plunge into a boiling pot and boil for 3 hours. Eat while very hot with Hard Sauce (see Index) or Soft Sauce (see below). Serves 8 generously.

Sister Amelia, North Union

SOFT SAUCE

1 CUP BUTTER

2 CUPS MAPLE OR BROWN SUGAR

2 TABLESPOONS ROSEWATER (SEE INDEX)

Cream butter with sugar, rolled fine; flavor with rosewater. Do not chill, for this will cool pudding.

The Legend of the Plum Pudding: "It is a tale which goes far back into the pagan times when the Celtic gods still lived in the hills of Britain. Daga was the god of plenty. When he saw the sun turn in its course to come closer to the earth with each lengthening day, he decided to hold a festival. So he built a great fire under an enormous cauldron called Undry. In the cauldron he placed the most delicious fruits of the earth and all other good things he cherished; there was meat and meal and fruit. Slowly he cooked it and spiced it and tasted it. Daga was pleased with this plum porridge and he was ready to rejoice at Yuletide."—From *Cooking for Christ,* by Berger.

SHAKER BOILED APPLES

6 BALDWIN APPLES

1 CUP COLD WATER

1/2 CUP SUGAR

Place fair-skinned apples, such as Baldwins or other good cooking apples, with only the cores removed, in a saucepan with about a half an inch of water. Pour over the apples about half a cup of sugar and boil until the apples are thoroughly cooked. Turn them carefully several times. Boil until the syrup turns thick as jelly. After one trial no one would have fair-skinned apples peeled. The skins contain a very

95

large share of the jelly-making substance and impart a flavor impossible to obtain otherwise. It is also said that a wise housekeeper instead of throwing away the skins and cores of sound pie apples would use them for jelly. A tumbler full of the richest sort can thus be obtained from a dozen apples when making pies (see Index, Apple Parings Jelly) .

Sister Marguerite, Canterbury

In Mary Whitcher's *Shaker Housekeeper,* published at Shaker Village (Canterbury) , New Hampshire, in 1882, we read: "About the nicest morsel that ever tickled the palate is a properly boiled apple; not boiled like a potato or steamed like a pudding" but prepared according to the recipe (above) sent by Sister Marguerite Frost of Canterbury. Sister Marguerite was for years a school teacher at Canterbury and is still very active. She contributed a number of the recipes in this volume.

"The supper was of hominy and plenty of rich milk, just set on the table in a shallow ten-quart pan. Such a repast, eaten in the light of a roaring fire, was pleasant enough in the simple long-ago. . . . In those days of the brick oven and the open fire, the corn tasted rich from the virgin soil and the creamy milk from the cows tasted from the honeysuckle they nibbled. . . . Age brings some of its most subtle illusions in the shape of food; the cold-storage turkey bears no resemblance to the gobbler of our childhood and there is something wrong with the buckwheat cakes of today!"—*Simplicity of Life in Old New England,* by Kate Wiggins.

Many of the Shaker Household Journals are pungent with the smells of the good earth—its fruits, succulent greens and scent-laden herbs.

SHAKER FLOATING ISLAND

1 TABLESPOON CORNSTARCH

1 QUART WHOLE MILK

5 EGGS, SEPARATED

1/2 CUP SUGAR

1/2 TEASPOON ROSEWATER OR VANILLA

1/4 TEASPOON SALT

3 TABLESPOONS SUGAR

Wet cornstarch with 2 tablespoons milk. Scald remaining milk. Into the well-beaten egg yolks stir moistened cornstarch and sugar. Pour scalded milk over egg mixture and heat gently over low flame, stirring constantly for 3 minutes. Add half of flavoring and pour into serving dish. Beat egg whites very stiff and add salt and 3 tablespoons of sugar and remainder of flavoring. Drop spoonfuls of this mixture into boiling water for 2 minutes. Remove by spoonfuls and float on custard. These are the islands. A favorite and very old recipe. Chill before serving. Serves 6.

Sister Marguerite, Canterbury

Quaint cooking terms found in very early Shaker Household Journals:

"Searce the sugar" referred to maple or brown sugar and meant sieve out all lumps and make fine.

"Pie Coffin" was a term used to define the case of the pie-shell.

"Cart an egg" meant beating it.

"Sallet," often used for a mixture of greens or a salad.

"Beat with birchen twigs" was a term used in the "wooden" era of Shaker cooking when wire beaters were scarce.

"Pompoon" was used for pumpkin.

"A gang of calves' feet" meant all four of the feet used at the time of butchering for calf-foot jelly—now known as gelatin.

"Butter the size of a walnut" was one of the first attempts at exact measurements.

Yours Kindly,
Mary Whitcher

Egg Dishes

From earliest times eggs were considered an important food for humans. To the Egyptian, for whom the goose was the most important source of meat, eggs were a staple food. They well understood the skill of artificial incubation of hen and goose eggs. Down through the ages mankind has turned to this important item of food.

Today we know that as far as vitamins are concerned, eggs are almost as rich a source as can be found. Nor are they lacking in essential proteins. Next to milk, eggs are our best protective food—but like milk must be supplemented by fruits and vegetables.

Eggs were an important item of diet with the Shakers, where dozens went daily into the making of custards, cakes, muffins, noodles, omelets and other dishes for their large families ranging from 80 to 100 members. Besides the many eggs consumed by the large households, the Sisters saw to it that the wide egg-baskets were well filled when the Shaker peddler made his weekly rounds. Baskets of eggs, pats of neatly molded butter, crocks of pickles and preserves were the Sisters' chief source of income for they, too, did their share in defraying the household expenses of the large establishments. This "egg money" was in turn spent for the ever-necessary lemons, nutmegs, pepper and salt and a few other items the self-sustaining communities could not raise.

In a Shaker Farm Journal at the Western Reserve Historical Society we read: "The average farmer is careless about his feathered flocks. All young crowers should be gotten ready for the pot, sold or exchanged for several roosters of some good outside flock in order to keep your stock from inbreeding. . . ."

When the ban was placed on meat-eating by the Mother Church in New Lebanon, egg dishes became a helpful substitute. In one little manuscript volume we find recipes for forty-one ways of "preparing substantial and tasty egg dishes," ranging from boiled, baked, coddled, battered and steamed to dropped, fried, smothered, frizzled, puffed and potted eggs, besides custards, soufflés and omelets.

The Shakers prided themselves on their thoroughbred herds; they also raised fine poultry—some famous as egg-producers, while others were raised because they made succulent, meaty pies, stews and broths. At North Union not only guinea fowls were raised, but pea-fowls also strutted about. There is no explanation given for raising these vain, haughty creatures except that they ornamented the enclosed garden about the Office of the Ministry and guest-house. The eggs of the guinea fowls were believed to be of a special fine flavor when hard-boiled and the flesh of the noisy, speckled little bird is a great delicacy.

Eggs are the most widely used of all foods because they can be used in so many different ways in dishes which are substitutes for meat—in baking and in desserts and beverages. Again, they are highly nutritious, the yolk being rich in vitamins. Eggs are used in thickening soups and sauces and as a coating for chops and croquettes when breaded. Eggs are also used for clarifying soups and coffee, as a stabilizer for fats in making salad dressing and mayonnaise and as a leavening agent in certain cakes and soufflés. As a garnish the hard-cooked, sliced egg or the riced yolk or chopped white is most useful. Eggs can be used in combination with a vast variety of foods, both as a stretcher of food, such as small quantities of meat, fish or vegetables converted into omelets and soufflés, or as a food binder in making croquettes and fritters. What finer leavener of food do we find than eggs when converted into Angel Food or Sponge Cake? When we take all these important properties of the humble little egg into consideration, it is small wonder that since the beginning of civilization philosophers have troubled their minds over which came first: the chicken or the egg?

It is claimed that the egg is the most universally used food in the world—that it is even more generally used than milk, upon which a religious ban has been placed in many Mohammedan lands where the cow is held sacred.

Although the Shakers knew nothing about the calories or the vitamins or the minerals which replenish and rebuild our bodies, their religion taught them to make the most of what they had at hand. The foods they produced on their large farms together with eggs, cheese and milk were an important part of their diet.

STUFFED EGGS

6 EGGS, HARD-COOKED

2 TEASPOONS BUTTER

1 TABLESPOON HEAVY CREAM

1/2 TEASPOON SALT AND PEPPER, MIXED

1 TEASPOON PREPARED MUSTARD

1/2 TEASPOON LEMON JUICE

1 EGG, UNCOOKED

1/2 CUP CRACKER CRUMBS

Cut the hard-cooked eggs in two, lengthwise; remove yolks. Pass the yolks through sieve and add butter, cream, salt and pepper, prepared mustard and lemon juice. Mix thoroughly and fill centers of egg halves and press them together. There will be a little of this mixture left over; add to whole egg and beat well. Roll stuffed eggs in mixture and then in cracker crumbs and fry in boiling fat until golden brown. Serves 6.   Mary Whitcher's *Shaker Housekeeper*

SHAKER DROPPED EGGS

6 EGGS

1/2 TEASPOON EACH SALT, VINEGAR

6 ROUNDS TOAST, BUTTERED

WHITE PEPPER

Lay muffin rings in the bottom of a skillet. Add 2 cups boiling water to which salt and vinegar have been added. Break eggs into the rings (which keep eggs nice and round); the vinegar tenderizes the whites. Just as soon as the whites set, remove egg and place on round of hot buttered toast. Sprinkle with white pepper and serve immediately. Very appetizing.

SPANISH EGGS

2 QUARTS BOILING WATER

1 TEASPOON SALT

1 CUP RICE, UNCOOKED

1 CUP TOMATO CATSUP

2 TABLESPOONS BUTTER

6 DROPPED EGGS (SEE ABOVE)

To the boiling water add salt and uncooked, washed rice, and cook until tender. Drain well and add catsup and butter; mix thoroughly. Reheat and put on hot platter; make six nests in rice and place hot dropped eggs in them. Garnish with water cress. Serves 6.

Mary Whitcher's *Shaker Housekeeper*

EGGS GOLDENROD

6 EGGS, HARD-COOKED

2 CUPS WHITE SAUCE (SEE INDEX)

6 SLICES TOAST, HOT BUTTERED

Slice fine the whites of the eggs and add to hot white sauce. Pour over hot toast and cover with yolks pressed through ricer. A good luncheon dish. Serves 6.

Amelia's Shaker Recipes

EGG CROQUETTES

6 EGGS, HARD-COOKED

1 TABLESPOON BUTTER

1 TABLESPOON FLOUR

3/4 CUP MILK

1/2 TEASPOON SALT

DASH PAPRIKA

1/2 CUP CRACKER CRUMBS

1 EGG, BEATEN

Chop eggs very fine. Melt butter in double boiler, blend in

flour gradually; add milk and season with salt and paprika. Stir until perfectly smooth. Add chopped eggs. Set aside to cool. When cold, shape into croquettes. Roll in cracker crumbs, then beaten egg and again in crumbs. Fry in deep fat until golden brown. Serves 6.

Shaker Household Hint: At the season when eggs are plentiful, pack them (small end down) in a box well filled with coarse salt, but never allow eggs to touch one another. Before packing have small holes bored in bottom of box to allow for any drainage of moisture. Some use oats instead of salt for storing eggs. Save all egg shells for settling coffee.

SHAKER SHIRRED EGGS

4 EGG WHITES

4 EGG YOLKS, KEPT WHOLE

SALT

PAPRIKA

1 TABLESPOON CHIVES, CHOPPED

Beat egg whites very stiff and put in buttered baking dish. With spoon make 4 openings in whites and slip in the unbroken yolks. Sprinkle with salt and paprika and bake 10 minutes in 350° oven. Top with chives and serve hot. Serves 4.   North Union

Shaker Household Hints:

Duck and goose eggs are very strong in flavor and should never be used in delicate cakes or custards. They are excellent, however for well-seasoned scrambled eggs or in Spanish omelet.

To soft cook an egg, three minutes is the allotted time.

To hard cook an egg, eight to ten minutes is required. Roll eggs about gently while cooking so yolk does not settle to one side. Immerse hard-cooked egg into cold water as soon as cooked; this will keep the shell from sticking to white.

Noodle-making was always an event at North Union, a Household Journal records: "Great heaps of flour and salt were sifted into the wide wooden bowls. Into a deep well in the center went countless eggs, for the noodles must be a rich yellow. When the dough was smooth and very thick it was formed into balls the size of an apple. These in turn were rolled into a round of dough about fifteen inches across and almost as thin as paper. A line was stretched back and forth over the cooking range. This was covered with fresh, clean cloth over which was draped the rounds of noodle dough to dry. These were watched carefully, for if the dough got too dry it would crack. When at just the right dryness, several of these rounds were laid on top of one another, rolled and cut very fine with a sharp knife. These freshly made noodles were very tasty and filling."

SISTER ABIGAIL'S BLUE FLOWER OMELET

4 EGGS

4 TABLESPOONS MILK OR WATER

1/2 TEASPOON SALT

1/8 TEASPOON PEPPER

1 TABLESPOON PARSLEY, MINCED

1 TEASPOON CHIVES, MINCED

12 CHIVE BLOOMS

2 TABLESPOONS BEST BUTTER

This delicious omelet can be made only when the chives are

in full bloom. Then take the eggs and beat them just enough to blend whites and yolks well. Add milk or water, seasoning, minced parsley and chives. Melt butter in a heavy iron skillet; pour in the mixture. When the edges of omelet begin to set, reduce the heat. With a pancake shovel slash uncooked parts until bottom is well browned. Then sprinkle the washed blooms over omelet and fold. Serve immediately on a hot platter. The blue blossoms add a delicious flavor and interest to the dish. Serves 4. North Union

When the fresh herbs were in season the Shaker cooks at North Union kept an assortment of herb-butters on hand. These were made by adding four tablespoons of finely minced herbs to a half-pound pat of fresh sweet butter. These delicious spreads were used on fresh homemade bread for their picnics and suppers, and were also used in flavoring vegetables or in giving that special touch to roasts and chops. Eggs and omelets fried in these herb-butters are delicious!

It is best to use sweet butter in making this delicacy, for salt draws the oils from the herbs and keeps them from forming a smooth mixture. Keep in small jars in your icebox or refrigerator; the North Union Shakers made them in pound lots and kept them in the spring-house.

SHAKER SUPPER OMELET

1/2 CUP BOILING MILK
1/2 CUP DRY BREAD CRUMBS
1 TEASPOON SALT
1/4 TEASPOON PEPPER
3 EGGS, BEATEN
1 TABLESPOON BUTTER

Pour boiling milk over bread crumbs. Let cool; add salt and pepper and mix in well-beaten eggs. Heat iron skillet and put in butter. When melted, turn in mixture and fry to golden brown on bottom. Fold over and serve at once. Never keep any egg dish waiting! Serves 2.   Union Village

DESSERT OMELET

4 SOUR APPLES

1/2 CUP SUGAR

1/2 TEASPOON NUTMEG

4 EGGS, WELL BEATEN

1 TABLESPOON BUTTER

Stew apples until soft and pass through sieve; add sugar and seasoning according to taste. Set aside to cool. When cold, add eggs and pour into well-buttered baking dish. Bake in a slow (250°) oven for 20 minutes. Serve warm with Cider Sauce (see below). Serves 4-6.   Sister Lettie

CIDER SAUCE

1 TABLESPOON BUTTER

3/4 TABLESPOON FLOUR

1 1/2 CUPS CIDER, BOILED DOWN

2 TABLESPOONS SUGAR

Blend butter and flour over low heat; add cider gradually, and stir smooth. Add sugar and boil 5 minutes. Serve hot.

107

QUAKER OMELET

3 EGGS, SEPARATED
1/2 TEASPOON SALT
1/8 TEASPOON PEPPER
1/4 TEASPOON MARJORAM, POWDERED
1 1/2 TABLESPOONS CORNSTARCH
1/2 CUP MILK
1 TABLESPOON BUTTER

Beat yolks of eggs well and add salt, pepper, marjoram, and cornstarch wet in milk. Heat an iron skillet. Now beat the egg whites stiff and add to mixture. Turn into buttered skillet. Cover tightly and place over low flame, so it will brown slowly but will not burn. It will take about 7 minutes. Fold and turn onto a hot platter and serve immediately. Serves 3.   Mary Whitcher's *Shaker Housekeeper*

SHAKER NOODLES

1 CUP BREAD FLOUR
1/2 TEASPOON SALT
1 TEASPOON SOFT BUTTER
1 EGG
3 TABLESPOONS WATER

Sift flour onto baking board. Form a well in center of flour and put in salt, butter, egg and water. Work into a stiff dough. Divide into three portions and roll each very thin. Place rolled dough on napkins and let dry about 15 minutes. Then stack one on top of the other and roll like jelly roll cake. Cut into very fine slices with sharp knife. Let dry a few minutes and boil in salted water. This makes a good substitute for potatoes. Serve with creamed meat or fish.

They are also good when boiled or fried and smothered with onions. Mary Whitcher's *Shaker Housekeeper*

Bread flour which contains more gluten than all-purpose flour should be used in making noodles; otherwise they may crumble. They may be cut in various widths. To add color and flavor to the dish, use juices, such as spinach or beet, in place of water.

Fish

Mary Whitcher's *Shaker Housekeeper* informs us that "fish can be a very delicious dish and it is a wholesome food when properly prepared, but only too often this delicate food is ruined in cooking, for very special care must be taken in neither over-cooking nor under-cooking fish."

The following extract from a Shaker Elder's Travel Journal while visiting North Union shows that the North Union Sisters were skilled in this delicate art of doing fish just to the right turn. "May 5th, 1837, and another real summer day! Last evening a number of the Brethren went fishing in Lake Erie. Toward noon today they brought home their catch—except the small ones which they always cast into their mill-pond on their way home. They had enough fish for all three Families [200 persons]; there were several muskies, a fine haul of white fish, a number of pike along with a lot of catfish and yet other kinds. They are all splendid eating. This evening we had a good supper of boiled catfish with herb-sauce, fried potatoes, boiled greens, pickled peppers, hot bread and lemon pie and tea. . . . May 8th. We have had fresh fish every day since we arrived and sometimes twice; they know we like it!"

The journal proceeds in the following manner: "May 9th. Another fine day. The Ministry took us to Cleveland. First of all, Eldress Betsy got herself a pair of spectacles. We then went up to the Light House. . . . Then down to the Shore near the pier where fishermen were drawing in their seine. We waited until they had made their draft of fishes which were not too numerous. Then we passed along the wharf which was a great experience—there lay steamboats, canal boats, schooners and one ship of perhaps 500 tons. We started home a little before noon and drove about four miles when we came to a dense woods off to the left [Kinsman Rd.] where we turned in, baited [fed] our horses while Eldress Vincy and Sister Lucy served up a fine dinner for us, 'in real Ohio fashion,' they claimed. In no time over a little fire they boiled potatoes, cooked fresh asparagus from their own garden and made 'Shaker Fish and Eggs' with even a kettle of tea in the bargain! It being almost three o'clock when our dinner was served we were quite hungry and ate every morsel with great relish. We reached home about six after a most comfortable and pleasant day."

This record shows that fish was an important item of diet at North Union, for in another Travel Journal we read: "May 4th, 1840. We arrived at North Union at six o'clock sharp and were heartily greeted in song by all the members of the community. In a brief time we were summoned to supper when we had a meal of fresh fish of excellent quality. This was the first meal of fresh fish we had had since leaving Pleasant Hill Community [Ky.] the first week in November."

Both these Journals were written during the Shaker ban on meat, which probably accounts for the abundance of fresh fish!

BOILED CATFISH

1 CATFISH, ABOUT 4 POUNDS

1 CARROT, DICED

1 TURNIP, DICED

1 ONION, DICED

4 SPRIGS PARSLEY

5 SOUP-PARSLEY ROOTS

SALT AND PEPPER

DASH OF TARRAGON

Catfish must be cooked when very fresh. Pour mild vinegar over it and sew the fish into a cheese cloth. Start vegetables boiling and add fish. Boil gently from 40 to 45 minutes. Remove cloth and serve very hot with hot Horseradish Sauce (see below). Serves 8.   North Union

HORSERADISH SAUCE

1 CUP WHITE SAUCE (SEE BELOW)

3 TABLESPOONS HORSERADISH, FRESHLY GRATED

1 TEASPOON SUGAR

2 TABLESPOONS VINEGAR

1/2 TEASPOON DRY MUSTARD

1/8 TEASPOON THYME, POWDERED

Mix in the order given and heat but do not boil. Serve hot with fish or meat.

ॐ   ॐ

WHITE SAUCE

2 TABLESPOONS BUTTER
2 TABLESPOONS FLOUR
2 CUPS MILK, WARM
SALT AND PEPPER

Melt butter and blend in flour over low heat; gradually blend in warm milk, and season. This sauce may be made by substituting fish stock in place of the milk. Or when used on delicately flavored vegetables, substitute water in which vegetable is cooked in place of milk.

ॐ   ॐ

Shaker Household Hints:

"The heads, back-bones and tails of fish should be cooked with a dash of marjoram and thyme and salt for half an hour and the liquid used in making sauces for fish or in chowders. Green onions and parsley stewed in butter and combined with two cups of fish broth and poured over two slightly beaten eggs make a delectable sauce for boiled or baked fish."

"Chervil, tarragon and mushrooms combined with lemon juice all make excellent flavorings for sauces served with fish."

"Catfish is extremely rich and fat, therefore boiling with vegetables is the best method of cooking it; the vegetables absorb some of the fatty flavor. It is a very interesting dish when thus prepared."

113

SHAKER BOILED FISH

3 POUNDS WHITEFISH OR FRESH MACKEREL
1 QUART WATER
2 TABLESPOONS CIDER OR WHITE WINE
1/2 TEASPOON CRUSHED PEPPERCORNS
1 STALK CELERY, CHOPPED
1 LARGE ONION, SLICED
2 CARROTS, SLICED

Boil water; add cider or wine, peppercorns, celery, onion and carrots. When broth is flavored and colored, add fish and cook until tender but not soft. Place fish on hot dish and serve with sauce made from the broth strained and poured over beaten eggs. Garnish with favorite fresh herbs —summer savory, thyme or tarragon are especially good with fish. North Union

SHAKER BAKED FISH

1 FISH, ABOUT 2 OR 3 POUNDS
6 SODA CRACKERS, CRUSHED
1 TEASPOON SALT
1 TABLESPOON PARSLEY, MINCED
1 TABLESPOON THYME, MINCED
1 TABLESPOON BUTTER
FISH BROTH TO MOISTEN
4 STRIPS SALT PORK
SALT AND CORNMEAL FOR DREDGING

Scrape fish well and wash; remove head and tail and simmer to make broth. Make a dressing of rolled crackers, salt, minced herbs and butter, and moisten with fish broth. Stuff the fish and fasten with skewers. Place in buttered baking dish and cut a few shallow slashes across fish. Lay on thin strips of salt pork and dredge with salt and cornmeal. Bake in slow (300°) oven for 1 hour. Serve on hot platter; surround with Tomato Sauce (see below) and wedges of lemon. Serves 4-6.

Mary Whitcher's *Shaker Housekeeper*

TOMATO SAUCE

8 MEDIUM-SIZED TOMATOES

4 CLOVES

1 TABLESPOON ONION, MINCED

2 TABLESPOONS BUTTER

2 TABLESPOONS FLOUR

SALT AND PEPPER

DASH OF CAYENNE PEPPER

MINCED PARSLEY

Cut tomatoes in quarters; put in stew pot and add cloves and onion, and stew for 15 minutes. Strain through sieve. Blend together butter and flour and stir into strained tomatoes. Add salt and pepper to taste and the dash of pepper. Sprinkle at last minute with parsley.

SHAKER FISH BALLS

2 CUPS COOKED FISH, CHOPPED

4 CUPS COOKED POTATOES, CHOPPED

2 EGG YOLKS, BEATEN

1 TABLESPOON PARSLEY, MINCED

SALT AND PEPPER

Use leftover fish. Measure and put into a wooden chopping

bowl, being careful no bones have been left in. Add to fish twice the amount of cold potatoes and chop together until very fine. Add egg yolks, minced parsley and salt and pepper to taste. Form into balls the size of a goose egg. Have a kettle of lard boiling and drop balls. Fry until golden brown. Slices of salt pork and milk gravy should be served with fish balls. This is a splendid supper dish. Serves 6.

Sister Lisett, North Union

SALT COD

Wash fish and soak in cold water overnight. In the morning pour off the water; put in fresh water and cook slowly. As soon as water comes to a boil, set pot on back of stove where it will keep hot but will not boil. Leave for 4 to 6 hours. The cod is now ready to be creamed or served on hot buttered toast; or it may be served with a sauce or fashioned into codfish balls.   Sister Lisett, North Union

SHAKER CODFISH BALLS

2 CUPS CODFISH, SHREDDED

2 CUPS RAW POTATOES, DICED

1 TABLESPOON BUTTER

1 EGG, BEATEN

DASH OF PEPPER

SUGGESTION OF NUTMEG

Cook the raw, salted codfish in boiling water with raw

potato until potato is done. Drain well and mash together. Then add butter, beaten egg, pepper and touch of nutmeg, but omit salt. Mix well. Have your lard or drippings boiling; drop in fish mixture by spoonful and fry to a golden brown. Do not soak the fish before boiling and do not mold into cakes, for this method makes them fluffier. Serve with oven-broiled bacon and a milk gravy. Serves 6.

Sister Lisset, North Union

"Few foods take as careful cooking as fish, for it must be thoroughly done but is very unappetizing if overdone."—Eldress Clymena

On consulting an old-timer, who had been raised by the North Union Shakers, of his childhood recreation, he remarked: "We had our fun just as all kids do who are brought up in a good home. What we boys liked best was fishing from the milldam of the Lower Lake after our chores were done. If our work was done well, we knew there was fun in store for us. The Lower Lake was well stocked, for the Brethren often went fishin' on Lake Erie all night, and when they came home with their catch in the morning, they always dumped the small fry in this Lake which was deep and well fed by springs and small creeks so the fish had plenty of food. We made our own fishin' gear, and no meals ever tasted better to us fellows than a mess of blue gills caught on the riggin' we made in the Boys' Shop. When these were cooked, just fresh and in plenty of Shaker butter such as you don't get these days, this was something to remember."

SHAKER FISH AND EGGS

2 CUPS RICH MILK OR LIGHT CREAM

1 TABLESPOON BUTTER

3 MEDIUM-SIZED BOILED POTATOES

1 CUP BOILED AND FINELY SHREDDED CODFISH

6 HARD-COOKED EGGS

1/4 TEASPOON SALT

1/8 TEASPOON PEPPER

Scald milk and add butter. In a buttered baking dish place a layer of sliced boiled potatoes; sprinkle with finely shredded boiled codfish, then with a layer of sliced hard-cooked eggs. Repeat and add seasoning and cover with heated milk. Simmer in slow (300°) oven for 25 minutes. Garnish top with minced hard-cooked eggs. Serves 6.

Mary Whitcher's *Shaker Housekeeper*

TURBOT IN CREAM

2-POUND BASS

1 PINT THIN CREAM

1 BUNCH PARSLEY

1 ONION

3 STALKS CELERY

2 TABLESPOONS FLOUR

4 TABLESPOONS BUTTER

BREAD CRUMBS

GRATED CHEESE

Boil the bass in salt water; flake it, removing all skin and bones. Scald the cream with parsley, onion and celery. Remove vegetables and thicken the cream with flour moistened in milk. Stir until smooth and add butter. Butter a deep

FISH

baking dish and put in a layer of fish and a layer of sauce. Repeat until dish is two-thirds filled. Cover top with a layer of fine bread crumbs and dust with grated cheese. Bake 30 minutes in medium (350°) oven. Serves 6.

Mary Whitcher's *Shaker Housekeeper*

CREAMED OYSTERS

A FEW THIN SLICES OF ONION
SEVERAL BLADES OF MACE
1 PINT LIGHT CREAM
1 TABLESPOON FLOUR
1/2 TEASPOON SALT
1/8 TEASPOON PEPPER
1 QUART OYSTERS

Put onion and mace in cream and simmer but do not boil. Mix flour with a little cold milk; add to cream and blend well. Skim out the mace and onion, and add salt and pepper. Add oysters and let come to a slight boil. Have rounds of hot buttered toast ready and serve oysters on toast. Serve with a bland cole slaw. Serves 4.

Mary Whitcher's *Shaker Housekeeper*

The peak of the oyster vogue in America was about 1840. "No evening of pleasure was complete without oysters; no host was worthy of the name who failed to serve them to his guests. In every town there were oyster parlors, oyster cellars, oyster saloons and oyster bars. . . . Oysters were sent inland as far as Cincinnati by the 'Oyster Express'—a light vehicle loaded with live oysters imbedded in straw kept wet with salt water. This transportation made the oysters expensive but throughout the east there were marts operated where for a shilling the customer was permitted to eat as many as he wished."—*The Way Our People Lived,* by W. E. Woodward

ട്ര   ട്ര

OYSTER STEW

4 TABLESPOONS BUTTER

1 PINT OYSTERS

2 CUPS HALF CREAM, HALF MILK

1/2 TEASPOON SALT

1/8 TEASPOON PEPPER

1 TABLESPOON PARSLEY, MINCED

1 TEASPOON CELERY LEAVES, MINCED

Melt butter, but do not brown; drain oysters and pour into butter and let come to boiling point. Set saucepan in a kettle of boiling water (or use double boiler), for oysters are delicate and direct heat toughens them. Pour on the milk and cream and add seasoning. When the oysters rise to the top, remove from heat. Sprinkle top with parsley and celery leaves, and serve very hot. Serves 2.   Union Village

ട്ര   ട്ര

FRIED OYSTERS

1 QUART OYSTERS

1 CUP CORNMEAL

SALT AND PEPPER

DASH OF POWDERED THYME

1 EGG, BEATEN

Drain oysters between towels; save liquid. Combine corn-meal with salt and pepper and a dash of thyme. Dip oysters in beaten egg, then in the cornmeal mixture. Fry in deep fat until golden brown. Put on very hot platter. Now mix oyster liquid with remaining meal mixture and drop by spoonfuls in the hot fat. Serve these mock oysters with the real; this adds interest to the dish. Serves 4-6.

OYSTER PIE

RICH PASTRY FOR 2 CRUSTS (SEE INDEX)
2 TABLESPOONS FLOUR
1 QUART OYSTERS
1 TEASPOON SALT
1/8 TEASPOON PEPPER
DASH OF THYME
2 1/2 TABLESPOONS BUTTER

Line a deep pie dish with pastry and dredge the bottom with flour. Drain oysters but save liquid. Place a layer of oysters on flour, season with salt, pepper and thyme; sprinkle with flour and dot with butter. Repeat and pour on oyster liquid. Cover with top crust. Bake in moderate (350°) oven for 30 minutes. Serves 4.   Shaker *Manifesto,* January, 1881

PICKLED OYSTERS

1 TEASPOON ALLSPICE
1 TEASPOON CLOVES
1 TEASPOON MACE
1/2 TEASPOON CINNAMON
2 CUPS MILD WINE VINEGAR
1 QUART LARGE OYSTERS

Mix spices together and add to vinegar; scald. When cold,

pour over oysters and let stand overnight. Next day scald the whole mixture for 1 minute. Chill well. This makes a good appetizer. Serves 4-6.

ટે   ૐ

SALMON LOAF

2 CUPS SALMON, COOKED OR CANNED
2 CUPS BREAD CRUMBS OR COOKED RICE
1/2 CUP MILK
2 EGGS, BEATEN
1 1/2 TABLESPOONS PARSLEY, MINCED
1 TABLESPOON MELTED BUTTER
1 TEASPOON SALT
1 TEASPOON LEMON JUICE

Flake salmon. Add all ingredients. Mold into loaf and put in buttered baking dish. Bake 40 minutes at 375°. Serves 4. Serve with Mushroom Sauce (see below).

ટે   ૐ

MUSHROOM SAUCE

2 TABLESPOONS BUTTER
1 CUP MUSHROOM CAPS, SLICED
SALT AND PEPPER TO TASTE
DASH OF SUMMER SAVORY
1 TABLESPOON FLOUR
1 CUP VEGETABLE OR BEEF STOCK

Heat pan and melt butter. Sauté mushrooms to a very light brown, for cooking them longer than 5 minutes toughens them. Season, add flour and stir well. Then add broth and stir until smooth. Serve hot.

ટે   ૐ

SCALLOPED TUNA

2 CUPS COOKED OR CANNED TUNA

2 TABLESPOONS BUTTER

4 TABLESPOONS FLOUR

1 CUP MILK

2 EGGS, BEATEN

1/4 TEASPOON PEPPER

1 TABLESPOON LEMON JUICE

1 TABLESPOON PARSLEY

1 TABLESPOON PIMIENTO

1/2 CUP BUTTERED BREAD CRUMBS

Flake tuna. Make a whitesauce of butter, flour and milk and after removing from heat gradually stir in eggs. Add seasoning, fish, lemon juice, parsley and pimiento and pour into buttered baking dish. Top with buttered crumbs. Bake at 375° for 25 minutes. Serves 4.

FRESH HALIBUT ON TOAST

2 CUPS FLAKED HALIBUT

2 TABLESPOONS BUTTER

2 TABLESPOONS FLOUR

1 CUP MILK, HEATED

1 CUP LIGHT CREAM

8 ROUNDS TOAST, BUTTERED

1 EGG, HARD-COOKED, CHOPPED

Cover fish with cold water and bring slowly to a boil. Drain well. Blend butter and flour and add heated milk and cream. When smooth add fish. Cook until liquid thickens. Serve on rounds of buttered toast. Garnish with chopped egg.

The original Herb House at New Lebanon, N.Y. Destroyed by fire in 1875.
(from an old print-Nordoff, '75)

Herbs

"In pottage without herbs there is neither goodness nor nourishment."—Litany. Today there are many fascinating books being written about herbs, such as *The Magic of Herbs, The Unprejudiced Palate, Herbs in Cookery* and a whole volume on Fine Herbs and others on Robust Herbs! Then, again, the Garden Clubs have awakened a tremendous interest—extending the length and breadth of our country—in these modest little plants which again are being raised in neat profusion in tiny plots beside many a kitchen door.

The modestly gray-clad or dull green plants with their inconspicuous blooms do not fill their important niches in the garden because of their beauty, but rather because of the time-honored service they have rendered man. In the

124

gray dawn of human history, shepherds and hunters used herbs to season their humble repast of meats half cooked over the open fires in field and forest. They learned these succulent greens transformed an ordinary morsel of food into a rare delicacy. Pliny, Horace and Virgil wrote of the use of herbs and the Bible mentions mint, rue and cumin. Herbs were among the first green plants cultivated in Europe and Asia, for down through the ages they were considered the key to all cures of human ailments.

Throughout the centuries every nationality developed a cookery which smacks of its favorite herb. Many early immigrants on arrival in America found new herbs, barks and roots awaiting their soup-pots and brew-kettles. These had been carefully tried out by the Red man, and many of them were adopted for use by the early settlers.

The early Shakers worked magic with herbs. Probably their greatest contribution to American cookery was their knowledge of herbs and their use in cooking. Herbs are a baffling subject, and it took a deal of experimenting to make their use practical and delightful. Food and herbs soon became inseparable to the Shakers. Their gardens were silver with marjoram, dainty with thyme and fragrant with the thorny rosemary; here rich herb-scents filled the air. The Sisters plucked into their flat, handwoven baskets the leaves and stems holding the secret, subtle flavors for foods and promising cures for the sick. These were delivered to the Brethren in the herb-house, who knew how to cure and care for herbs.

In several of the Shaker communities, where they raised herbs for commercial use (New Lebanon, South Union and Harvard), these herb-houses were large structures well equipped with counters, dryers, distillers and grinders. Down the center extended long work counters where the finished produce was boxed, packaged and labeled for home and foreign consumption. We read in their journals that "the air in the herb-houses was filled with the cozy scent of pot-pourri and sweet lavender from countless bunches lying in flat herb-baskets. . . . Herbs are cut in the middle of summer just before they bloom. . . ."

The Shakers advocated the use of herbs in cookery be-cause "they stimulate appetite, they give character to food and add charm and variety to ordinary dishes." The Shakers sent out circulars with some of their large orders, giving di-rections on "how to use these herbs which give such refresh-ing, delicate odors and flavors to food."

The pioneer, on a heavy salt-meat diet with scant sugar supply and spices at a prohibitive price, craved these green herbs which made his few root vegetables more palatable. Herbs were never a luxury; they belonged to the diet of both the king and the commoner, both the rich and the poor. They can be raised in a tiny plot at the kitchen door of any cottage or even in a pot on the window sill.

In the *Herb Grower Magazine* of Spring, 1951, there is an article by Sister Marguerite Frost of Canterbury, New Hampshire, on "Shaker Herbs and Herbalists." She states: "The Shakers were among the first people in this country to gather wild herbs and roots for sale. In the earliest days of the Shakers, as was true of all rural dwellings, it was neces-sary to do something to earn some money, for not quite every necessity could be produced on the farm. What could have been more logical than to search the woods and fields for the herbs that everyone used for medicine and to develop those not found growing wild? Would that you might have seen the Marigolds, Poppies, Foxgloves, Feverfew, Lobelia, Yellow-dock and other plants growing in this garden at Canterbury.

"For years Thomas Corbett was the efficient doctor of the Shaker community at Canterbury, New Hampshire. . . . He built up a large and proficient herb business."

Elder Freeman White, also of the Canterbury community, contributed to the Shaker Herb Culture. "He had gained much knowledge of medical lore from the Indians when a young man," Sister Marguerite's article informs us.

The Harvard, Massachusetts, Shaker community and the New Lebanon, New York, Shaker community both specialized in the growing and preparation of medicinal and culinary herbs, and sold enormous quantities both in this country and in Europe. In a single year (1849-1850) the Harvard community "pressed 10,150 pounds of herbs and roots." Canterbury, Sabbathday Lake, Union Village and South Union communities were all such large producers of herbs that each built a spacious herb-house to handle this lucrative business. Wagonloads of rose blooms were stacked in the herb-houses at Union Village in season, where acres of damask roses were raised for the sole purpose of being converted into rosewater and extract.

SPINACH WITH ROSEMARY

2 POUNDS SPINACH
1/4 TEASPOON FRESH ROSEMARY, MINCED
1 TEASPOON PARSLEY, CHOPPED
1 TABLESPOON GREEN ONION, CHOPPED
2 TABLESPOONS BUTTER
SALT AND PEPPER TO TASTE

Wash the spinach 3 or 4 times to rid it of all grit and sand. Chop rather fine and place in a heavy iron pot. Add herbs and butter and cover well; let simmer in its own juice until tender (about 15 minutes). Remove cover and add salt and pepper. Serve very hot. Serves 4.   Amelia's Shaker Recipes

Rosemary is that choice herb which has a beautiful Biblical legend associated with its fragrance. It was in the long ago when Mary and Joseph took the Holy Infant into Egypt, that the Virgin Mother hung His freshly washed garments upon the drab, bristly desert shrub to dry. So great was the gratitude of the little shrub for the holy touch bestowed upon it, that it has ever since borne the sweet fragrance of the Infant's robes.

In the olden days the churches of Europe were garlanded in rosemary for weddings and the great festivals. The herb was also cast into the open grave at burials and worn in the boot of the bride at nuptials. Today we often combine it with chives, parsley or thyme. It is especially good used in dressing for fowl and veal, and is excellent for flavoring drinks.

Chervil is a close relative of parsley; so delicate is its flavor that it can be used generously in salads, soups and sauces. It is excellent combined with chives, minced fine and sprinkled over cottage cheese, cream cheese balls or slices of Yankee cheese. Chop it fine and use it in any green salad.

STRING BEAN SALAD

2 CUPS COOKED STRING BEANS

2 CUPS LETTUCE, SHREDDED

2 GREEN ONIONS, MINCED

2 SPRIGS SUMMER SAVORY

6 NASTURTIUM LEAVES

12 NASTURTIUM PODS

SALT AND PEPPER TO TASTE

ANY FAVORITE DRESSING

Mix the cold, boiled green beans with the shredded lettuce. Mince the green onion (top and all) over beans. Add the minced summer savory and nasturtium leaves and pods. Season with salt and pepper and toss with favorite dressing. Serves 4.   Amelia's Shaker Recipes

There are fine herbs and robust herbs. The robust kind are the practical, highly flavored herbs such as borage, sage, the mints, summer and winter savory, dill, fennel and horseradish. Summer savory adds delicate flavor to the strong vegetables, such as cabbage, Brussels sprouts and cauliflower. It is especially good with turnips or with dried peas. A generous sprinkling of summer savory a-top a bowl of potato soup will long be remembered! Also try it in a green vegetable salad!

One of my strongest and most delightful childhood gustatory memories is that of the heavy, woolly, tasty borage leaves cut into paper-thin strips, generously distributed in my grandmother's "wilted leaf-lettuce salad!" So great is my pleasure at the recollection of this unusual taste sensation, that since grown I have never dared partake of it. Why shatter complete satisfaction? I travel miles each spring to buy a plant of borage and throughout the long summer just stand and admire its fuzzy, heavy leaves and am wholly satisfied in just remembering how it tasted long, long ago!

BEEF STEW WITH HERBS
LUMP OF SUET
1 POUND BONELESS BEEF,
  CUT IN SERVING PIECES
1 TABLESPOON FLOUR
1 TEASPOON SALT
1/4 TEASPOON PEPPER
1 LARGE ONION, SLICED
1/2 CUP CIDER
1/2 CUP WATER
1/4 TEASPOON MARJORAM, MINCED
1/2 TEASPOON THYME, MINCED
2 CARROTS, DICED
2 TURNIPS, DICED

129

Cut suet fine and try it out in an iron pot. Remove cracklings. Roll chunks of meat in flour, salt and pepper and brown well in hot fat. Add onion and simmer with meat for 10 minutes. Add cider and water; cover pot tightly and let cook very slowly for 2 hours. Add a few drops of liquid from time to time, if needed. Last half hour add minced herbs, diced carrots and turnips. Taste to see if seasoned satisfactorily. Simmer until vegetables are tender. Serves 2.

North Union

The fine herbs are so distinct in their perfume that often they have to be toned down or blended with other herbs; basil, thyme, marjoram, chervil and chives belong to this class.

Basil "blesses all food that it touches." The fresh basil is good from earliest spring to late fall. It is good in soups, salads, fruit drinks, cheeses and egg dishes. Or put it in with boiled vegetables. Chop it fine and sprinkle it over chops just before serving; it transforms any dish to something new and different. Pot it in late fall and bring it into the kitchen.

Marjoram is a great favorite with cooks. It is used in stews and soups and in scalloped potatoes or with cold slaw or over boiled turnips. It is especially good in turkey dressing. Pot the plant for winter use.

SHAKER STUFFING FOR CHICKEN

3 TABLESPOONS BUTTER

2 MEDIUM ONIONS, MINCED

3 CUPS DRIED BREAD CRUMBS

1/2 CUP CELERY LEAVES, CHOPPED

1 TABLESPOON SUMMER SAVORY, CHOPPED

1 TEASPOON BASIL, CUT FINE

1 TEASPOON FRESH THYME

1 TEASPOON SALT

1/8 TEASPOON PEPPER

10 CHESTNUTS

1/2 CUP HOT WATER

3 TABLESPOONS BUTTER

Melt butter; sauté onion but do not brown; add to bread crumbs. Add all herbs, salt and pepper. Blanch chestnuts and cut in quarters. Add to dressing. Heat water and add butter and mix well into dressing. Stuff chicken and truss well. Rub the skin with soft butter and dust with salt.

Eldress Clymena

In ancient Greece where the bees gathered wild thyme, the honey was flavored with this sweet herb. In Switzerland and Germany the goats' milk cheese also savored from the wild thyme. "Any cook who knows her herbs is never without thyme."—North Union

Parsley is too frequently used only as a garnish. It is essential in soups and sauces and is especially good in hot fish sauce. Or mince it fine and sprinkle over any hot dish of meat, fish or vegetables; it never fails to impart a subtle flavor which adds joy to living.

In the Middle Ages herbs had many uses; as flavoring for food, in perfume-making, in concocting love potions and as medicines and also as incense on altars.

In a day when there was no refrigeration, herbs were essential in flavoring meats. Even today with excellent refrigeration most dishes can be improved by the subtle use of such herbs as basil, chervil, parsley, borage and rosemary. Try them!

SHAKER ROSEWATER

When the roses, red or damask ones preferred, are at their best, pluck off the petals from fresh blooms. Do not use fallen petals or faded blooms. To every peck of petals use a quart of fresh spring water. Put this in a cold still over a very low fire and distill slowly. Distill it a second time. Bottle the rosewater and cork loosely and let stand 3 days. Then fasten the cork down tightly and let age before using.

North Union

Commercial rosewater can be obtained at certain drug-stores. Be sure to ask for the food-flavoring rosewater, not the hand-lotion type which is loaded with glycerin.

Sister Marguerite Frost of Canterbury gives the following instructions for preparing rose petals for Shaker Rosewater: "Gather the roses in full bloom and to every pound of petals add four ounces of salt. Put them in an earthen vessel or clean vat and let them remain until thoroughly saturated with salt." Distill as above directed.

She adds further: "Rosewater is an excellent remedy for sore eyes and is equally good in flavoring pies, cakes, puddings and custards."

From Spring Issue, 1951, *Herb Grower Magazine*

"The rose bushes at Mt. Lebanon Shaker community were planted along the sides of the roads which passed through our villages and were greatly admired by passers-by. It was strictly impressed upon the younger Sisters that a rose was valuable for its usefulness rather than for its beauty; it was not intended to please us with its color and perfume alone, but by its mission, which was to be made into rose-water used in flavoring certain foods and to keep in store for the infirmary where liberal quantities went into bathing an aching head or feverish body. We used only crimson roses, as they were supposed to make a stronger-flavored water than the paler varieties."—Sister Marcia, Mt. Lebanon

SHAKER HERB HINTS

Spiced salt should always be kept on hand; it is easily made by mixing 1 1/2 teaspoons each of powdered thyme, bay leaf, black pepper and nutmeg with 3/4 teaspoon of cayenne pepper and marjoram to which you add 3 teaspoons powdered cloves. Sift these together and put in a tightly closed canister. To this add 3 teaspoons salt. Keep canister well closed. This is an outstanding seasoning for soups, dressings and meats.—North Union

Mint: Often used in disinfecting sick rooms.

Mint Sauce: Carefully wash and chop a cup of mint leaves. Cover with a cup of good vinegar. Add a tablespoon sugar and a dash of salt and pepper. Serve in a small pitcher with lamb roast or chops. It can be made of fresh mint in the summer and bottled for winter use.

Sage: Probably the most domesticated of all herbs, it is used the world over in sausages and with duck or goose.

Mustard: Its seeds are both white and black or dark. The seed contains a great amount of oil which gives it the pungent odor and taste. It is often used as a household remedy by the Shakers. When mixed with warm water it is an effective emetic, while a hot mustard foot-bath was believed to avert a cold. A mustard plaster applied to a sick chest was also an effective remedy.

Poppies: Great quantities of these flowers were raised by the Shakers in their many herb gardens. They were not raised for the beauty of their silken petals but for their tiny seeds used in flavoring small cakes and rolls. They also sold them for bird seed. The seed contains a rich oil.

Feverfew: This herb was steeped and used for stomach aches.

Geranium: Used in flavoring soaps and also mouth washes.

Rose Geranium: Used in flavoring bland jellies.

Borage minced fine and added to an early spring salad adds great joy to life; the fuzzy little leaf with its cucumbery flavor is a real taste-thrill in early spring.

The Shakers advised the use of freshly plucked herbs whenever possible. When the fresh are not available, use only about one-third the amount of the dried, for they are truly potent if properly prepared.

"Variety is essential in diet! A constant diet of even the choicest roast beef would soon pall on one!" This is the office of herbs—to give variety to staple foods, especially during the long winter when our forebears lived on root vegetables and salted meats.

Through the addition of celery seed and caraway, chives and parsley, even the common Irish potato appeared in eighteen different roles at North Union.

With string beans—use parsley, basil or summer savory.

With cabbage and its large family—use sweet marjoram.

With carrots—chives, parsley or chopped mint are recommended.

With most any vegetable a dash of tarragon brings forth new wonders!

Meats

A chapter on meat and meat cookery reads very differently today from one written in the early days of Shakerism. Segregated slaughter- and packing-houses, refrigeration, and meat counters as artistically arranged as a floral exhibition, have all aided in removing the grim and ghastly reality of home-butchering which was once so essential a part of rural life a century ago! Yea, even in the quiet peaceful villages of the gentle-hearted Shakers! Every fall on a frosty day in late November, the butcher knives were sharpened to a razor-edge, the mighty scalding cauldrons were gotten in readiness, the crude meat-grinders and sausage-guns were brought forth, and rows of huge earthen crocks, barrels and kegs were thoroughly cleansed and filled with brine (stout enough to float an egg) , awaiting the time when the surplus stock of the farm was converted into hams, corned brisket, sausage and tempting flitches of bacon.

Sometimes the itinerant butcher performed this gruesome task, but usually it was taken care of by some of the Brethren behind a distant barn screened from sight of the Sisters and children. This autumn kill was a necessity, an essential part of rural life. If the pioneer Shaker wanted sustenance for his body, enabling him to perform his heavy labor and to go forth daily in his religious dance, corned-beef hash and pickled spare-ribs and sausages must be supplied and prepared for the table! Cooking fats, especially, were in constant demand among the frontiersmen. Nothing could be baked or fried without suitable fats. Between the years 1630 and 1740 it was an established rule that all immigrants who came to these shores must bring with them a gallon of oil or pure fats. The pioneers' candles and soap also wholly depended upon fats.

While the Shaker Brethren were dividing up the carcasses into suitable cuts, herbs and spices were weighed and measured by the Sisters to give savor to sausage and tang to bologna. When saltpeter was available for curing meats, the older children ground it on the hominy block. Then hams and shoulders were laid in criss-cross fashion in great barrels of sugar-cure awaiting the day when they would be suspended from the rafters of the smoke-house, where tiny fires of hickory chips or green corncobs were smoldering in iron pots. These smoldering embers imparted aroma and pungent flavor to the ripening viands.

Deep down in the coolest of their large cellars were barrels of corned-beef and rows of crocks of herb-laden sausages and huge tubs of lard often delicately scented with leaf of bay or thyme. Yea, the Shakers who abhorred waste used every fragment of the kill—the feet of veal or pork were fashioned into dainty jelly or gelatin dishes for the aged and infirm; the heads were boiled and converted into appetizing loaves of scrapple or head-cheese, so tasty for breakfast on frosty mornings. The tripe, kidneys and liver went into aromatic stews and succulent dinner dishes, while the hearts, jowls, sweetbreads and brains were disguised into toothsome pressed meats encased in jelly. Even the bladder was blown up and given to the children as a new ball, while the curly pigtail was salvaged and hung beside the Shaker Brethrens' workbench to grease their saws.

For several days following the sad event, the great Shaker kitchens thrice daily belched forth the pungent aroma of roasts, steaks and chops being prepared with rosemary, thyme and summer savory. These fresh meats had to be eaten almost immediately in a day when refrigeration was unknown. These feasts of fresh meats were followed by months of salted, dried and smoked meats. The Shaker Sisters were mighty ingenious in contriving countless ways of adding variety to this limited cuisine. Chickens, rabbits, an occasional wild turkey or a joint of venison at times brought relief from the monotonous salt-meat diet.

We read that in the Kentucky Shaker communities "the Brethren went a-hunting for Christmas dinner in 1820." We also read that they often went a-fishing in the nearby rivers. Here, in the wilds overlooking Cleveland, "the wild turkeys strutted along Turkey Lane [now Overlook Road] as late as 1830."

"Thy folds shall be full of sheep . . ." Psalm 65.

SHAKER HOG'S HEAD CHEESE

1 QUART COOKED, CHOPPED PORK

2 CUPS STOCK

1 TEASPOON SALT

1/4 TEASPOON PEPPER

1/2 TEASPOON CLOVES, GROUND

1/3 CUP SAGE LEAVES, MINCED

Take the head and heart of freshly killed pork. In order to cleanse thoroughly, remove ears, eyes, snout and brains by splitting. Soak head and heart in cold water to extract blood, or the cheese will be cloudy and dark in color. Cover with water and cook until meat falls from bones. Drain and save 2 cups of stock. Dice meat, add stock, salt, pepper, cloves and sage leaves. Mix thoroughly and cook 1/2 hour. Pack into crocks with straight sides; insert a plate over it and weight down well. In two or three days this will be ready to be turned out of crock, sliced down and served cold for supper with horseradish or mustard. Very delicate and delicious.

Sister Abigail, North Union

Tremendous labor was involved in putting up the season's meat supply. The lard had to be "tried out"—rendered or melted down and stored in airtight containers. This was often delicately flavored with rose geranium leaves, a sprig of thyme or even a whisp of rosemary. In order to keep the smoked and salted meats from spoiling, the spring-house and cellars had to be well ventilated.

Even the "cracknels" left over from trying out the lard were never wasted. The Shaker records state: "Put them into a pot of boiling salted water and thicken with cornmeal." This could be baked as "crackling bread" or sliced and fried as mush.

MEATS

SHAKER FLANK STEAK

3 POUNDS FLANK STEAK

2 TABLESPOONS BUTTER

2 ONIONS, CHOPPED

1 TEASPOON SALT

1/8 TEASPOON PEPPER

JUICE OF 1/2 LEMON

2 TABLESPOONS CELERY, MINCED

2 TABLESPOONS CARROT, MINCED

2 TABLESPOONS GREEN PEPPER, MINCED

2 TABLESPOONS FLOUR

1/4 CUP TOMATO CATSUP

2 CUPS BOILING WATER

A flank steak has long fibers, therefore cut or score with a sharp knife. Melt butter in an iron skillet and sear meat. Add lemon juice, then the chopped vegetables and seasonings. Put all ingredients on top of steak. Dredge with flour. Pour boiling water around steak and cook in a slow oven (200°) for 2 1/2 hours. Its own rich gravy will be formed. This is a delicious way to fix a cheap cut of meat. Serves 6.

Amelia's Shaker Recipes

With our deep freeze and modern meat markets, the mention of the Shaker smoke-houses does not even suggest an image to the average reader! However, they were very real and significant to the Shakers and to our forefathers. At North Union the smoke-house was the first brick building ever erected in that community. The gentle Brethren even made their own bricks under the supervision of Brother Prentiss who had learned the trade Down East. This building was not very large but was very snug and air-tight in order that none of the fumes of the smoldering hickory be wasted!

ROAST OF PORK

5 OR 6 POUNDS ROAST OF PORK
JUICE OF 1/2 LEMON
1/8 TEASPOON GROUND GINGER
1 TEASPOON FLOUR
1 TEASPOON SALT
DASH OF PEPPER

Trim off some of the fat, for much fat spoils the flavor of any meat and makes pork indigestible. Place roast in baking pan and pour over it the lemon juice. Dust with ginger; sprinkle with salt and pepper and dredge with flour. Bake in a slow oven (250°) for 3 hours. Last half hour surround roast with small peeled potatoes. These will absorb some of the fat. Make a brown gravy from the pan leavings. Serves 8.

North Union

HOW TO COOK SALT PORK

"At certain seasons it is hard to procure fresh meat, and salt pork becomes a steady diet for weeks at a time, therefore it is well to know how to cook it in sundry ways and avoid monotony of diet. If only a little thought and care is given to the matter, salt pork can be made a palatable dish. The proper way to fry it is to boil it first for 10 minutes. When cold remove rind and cut in neat slices 1/4 inch thick—roll in cornmeal and fry to a golden crisp. Or broil it over the live coals of the stove which gives it a delicious flavor. Yet another tasty mode makes it a most satisfactory dish; fry the strips partly and then dip them into a batter of eggs and flour and fry in a well-buttered skillet. Or, cut the bacon in thick slices and bake them with your beans. Again, place thin slices on the succotash and brown in the oven. Vary your vegetables as much as possible; also your sauces, relishes and salads as well as your desserts and this will all help to relieve the monotony of a salt-pork diet." Early Union Village

ROAST WILD TURKEY

DRESSED TURKEY, ABOUT 12 POUNDS
2 LOAVES WHITE BREAD, SLICED
1 CUP MELTED BUTTER
1 CUP HOT WATER
2 CUPS CHESTNUTS, COOKED AND CHOPPED
SALT AND PEPPER TO TASTE
1 TEASPOON SWEET MARJORAM, POWDERED
1 TEASPOON THYME, MINCED

Pluck bird thoroughly; then scrub with a brush and wash inside and out. Stuff breast and body with sliced and slightly toasted bread, broken into small pieces to which is added melted butter, hot water, cooked and chopped chestnuts, salt and pepper to taste and sweet marjoram and thyme. Stuff bird and sew up well, so flavors do not escape. Truss the bird and cover with soft butter and sprinkle with cornmeal. Dust with salt and pepper. Bake in a moderate oven (300°) for 4 1/2 hours; baste often. Serve with cranberry sauce, creamed turnips, whipped squash and steamed dumplings, which are delicious with turkey gravy. South Union

In the early history of Shakerism in the west, wheat was often very scarce and the breast meat of baked wild turkey was often used as a substitute for bread.

Salt was another scarce commodity in the early days of

the western Shaker communities. Salt sold in the Western Reserve in the early days for as high as $20.00 a barrel, until salt mines were opened in Ohio.

ॐ   ॐ

SISTER CONTENT'S HASH

2 CUPS COLD COOKED MEAT, DICED

1 CUP COLD COOKED POTATOES

1/2 CUP ONION, DICED

1/3 CUP GREEN PEPPER, DICED

1 CUP LEFTOVER GRAVY

SALT AND PEPPER

1 TABLESPOON BUTTER

DASH PAPRIKA

1/4 CUP BREAD CRUMBS

1/2 TABLESPOON CHEESE, GRATED

No household can be run economically without serving hash occasionally. Nor is there a dish for which there are fewer rules in making, for hash is just what the word implies— putting together whatever is at hand or left over and it must, at times, be left to the cook's imagination. For those who lack imagination the above suggestion may serve as a guide, which may be varied in dozens of ways. To make this dish inviting, it is best to dice or chop all ingredients instead of passing through a grinder, which mashes and blends food too much. Butter a baking dish and add the ingredients, except bread crumbs and cheese, and blend well. Sprinkle top with bread crumbs and dust with grated cheese or dot with butter. Brown well in a moderate (350°) oven. Beaten eggs can be added and hash formed into balls or patties and fried. Or it can be fried like an omelet.

୫ଇ   ୫୫

CORNED BEEF AND CABBAGE

4 POUNDS CORNED BEEF
6 POTATOES
6 TURNIPS
6 CARROTS
6 ONIONS
1 SMALL CABBAGE, CUT IN 6 PARTS

Soak choice brisket of corned beef in cold water for an hour. Drain and cover with fresh cold water and bring to boil. Skim well. Shove pot to back of stove and let meat simmer very gently for 4 hours; 30 minutes before meat is done, boil, in a separate pot, the peeled potatoes, turnips, carrots and onions, salted lightly. In still another pot cook the cut cabbage 15 minutes. Lift the brisket onto a large, well-heated platter and surround with the cooked vegetables. Serve with fresh horseradish or mustard.

୫ଇ   ୫୫

The origin of the word "corned" when applied to the delicately tender, crimson meat is interesting. Before the discovery of North America and its Indian maize (now known as corn), the word corn meant grain. In 1550 the manufacturers of gun powder used the term "corned" to indicate their product had been spread out and allowed to dry in grains. Shortly after that the term "corned" was applied to beef that had been sprinkled with grains of salt in order to preserve it.

୫ଇ   ୫୫

143

HAM BAKED IN CIDER

11-POUND HAM

24 CLOVES, WHOLE

1 CUP BOILING WATER

1 QUART CIDER

2 TABLESPOONS BROWN SUGAR

2 SMALL ONIONS

1 TABLESPOON LEMON JUICE

1 TABLESPOON FLOUR, BROWNED

Scrub ham thoroughly and soak overnight in cold water. If the ham has been precooked, it will be ready for baking. If not, put in cold water and bring to rapid boil; reduce heat and simmer for 3 hours. Let cool in liquid. Remove rind and trim fat; sear and stud with cloves. Combine boiling water, cider, brown sugar and onions and boil 10 minutes. Strain and pour over ham in roaster and bake 1 hour in moderate oven, basting every 15 minutes. Strain liquid; add lemon juice and thicken with browned flour. Serve this as sauce with ham.

SHAKER BEEF STEW

4 POUNDS STEW BEEF

3 TABLESPOONS BUTTER

SALT AND PEPPER

FLOUR FOR DREDGING

2 QUARTS BOILING WATER

2 POUNDS SMALL POTATOES, PEELED

5 GOOD-SIZED ONIONS

1 PINT CARROTS, PEELED

1 PINT TURNIPS, PEELED AND HALVED

3 BLADES CELERY

Cut stew beef in 2-inch squares. Melt butter in iron pot and sear meat. Dredge meat with salt, pepper and flour. Add boiling water and simmer for 3 hours. Add potatoes, onions, carrots, turnips and celery. Add more flour thickening, if necessary, and simmer for 30 minutes. Have dumpling mixture ready (see below) and drop into stew by spoonfuls. Cover tightly and cook 12 minutes more. Serves 6-8.

Mary Whitcher's *Shaker Housekeeper*

DUMPLINGS
2 CUPS FLOUR, SIFTED
6 TEASPOONS BAKING POWDER
1 TEASPOON SALT
2 EGGS
MILK, ABOUT 3/4 CUP
2 CUPS STOCK

Sift flour with baking powder and salt. Break eggs into cup and fill with milk; beat well and mix into dry ingredients. Heat stock in a 12 inch skillet and bring to a boil. Dip spoon into stock, then fill with batter and drop into stock. Do not cook too many at a time; dumplings must not touch. Cover tightly and cook 2 minutes. Turn dumplings and cook 2 minutes longer. Serve very hot with gravy.

VENISON ROAST
4-POUND VENISON ROAST
1/2 CUP MILD VINEGAR
1 CUP FLOUR PASTE, THICK
2 TABLESPOONS SOFT BUTTER
SALT AND PEPPER TO TASTE
4 TABLESPOONS CURRANT JELLY
JUICE OF 1 LEMON

Take a haunch (4 pounds) of venison; soak in mild vinegar for several days, turning frequently. Dry well and cover over with thick paste made of flour and water. Bake in medium (350°) oven for 2 hours. Remove paste and rub well with butter. Sprinkle with salt and pepper and dredge lightly with flour. Bake 30 minutes in hot oven, basting with butter frequently. Season pan gravy with currant jelly and the juice of a lemon. Serve piping hot with mashed turnips and glazed sweet potatoes.   South Union

There are recipes for fried rabbits, hare soup, venison steaks and hare pot-pie in the early cooking annals of the Shakers. In a modern work on "Food Shortages in the World," it is suggested that if every American home substituted a rabbit for steaks or chops once weekly, the meat supply of the world would be tremendously stretched! Rabbit or hare if soaked in very mild vinegar for several hours or overnight, or better yet in white wine, is just as delicious as chicken when properly cooked. It can be substituted for chicken in almost any good recipe—but remember to soak it first!

ROAST GUINEA HEN

1 YOUNG HEN
2 CUPS BREAD CRUMBS
1 CUP CELERY LEAVES, MINCED
1 TEASPOON SALT
2 TABLESPOONS BUTTER
JUICE OF 1/2 LEMON
1/2 CUP HOT WATER
2 EGG YOLKS, BEATEN
1 CUP CREAM
SALT AND PEPPER

Mix bread crumbs, celery leaves, salt and butter, and stuff bird with mixture. Rub bird with part of lemon juice and place in roaster. Baste with water and remainder of lemon juice. Cover tightly and roast in moderate oven 1 hour. Pour off juice and thicken by blending with beaten egg yolks, cream, salt and pepper, blended well. Pour over bird and bake 30 minutes longer, uncovered. Serves 3-4.

North Union

SHAKER FRIED CHICKEN

2 SPRING CHICKENS, QUARTERED

3 TABLESPOONS SOFT BUTTER

1 TABLESPOON PARSLEY, MINCED

1 TEASPOON MARJORAM, MINCED

2 TABLESPOONS FLOUR

2 TABLESPOONS BUTTER

2 TABLESPOONS LARD

SALT AND PEPPER

1 CUP LIGHT CREAM

Select chickens weighing 2 1/2 pounds or a little over, for smaller ones lack flavor and cook up waxy. Wash well and quarter. Rub thoroughly with soft butter and sprinkle generously with parsley and marjoram. Let stand for 1 hour. Then roll in flour to which salt and pepper has been added. Heat an iron skillet (or any preferred kind) and add butter and lard combined. Cook chicken on all sides until golden brown. Pour cream over and let simmer, covered, for 20 minutes. Serve with water cress and a tasty salad.

Eldress Clymena Miner

SISTER LETTIE'S VEAL LOAF

6 HARD CRACKERS, GROUND FINE

3 EGGS

1 CUP RICH MILK

3 POUNDS VEAL GROUND

1/2 POUND PORK, GROUND

2 TEASPOONS SALT

1/4 TEASPOON PEPPER

1 TEASPOON CELERY SEED

2 TABLESPOONS SOFT BUTTER

Roll the crackers to fine crumbs. Beat eggs and add milk. Mix all ingredients together thoroughly. Shape into long roll. Place in roaster and dot with butter. Bake at 225° for 2 hours, basting frequently. Make gravy by browning some flour in iron skillet, then blend with loaf leavings in bottom of pan. Use potato water or milk for mixing gravy. Serves 8.

Shaker Housekeeping Journal Hints:

"Never throw away the water in which vegetables have been cooked. Always use as little water in cooking vegetables as possible. This pot-liquor or vegetable water contains nourishment and flavor and should be used in making gravys, sauces and stews." (Today we know that these waters are rich in vitamin content, and good cooks carefully salvage them for many uses just as our Shaker sisters did many years ago.)

Rice and barley water are also good binders for sauces and gravy.

Never cook your minced herbs longer than 20 minutes; they loose their flavor and aroma.

Never use milk or cream in herb sauces, for the delicate flavor of the herb can not compete with the heavy flavor of cooked milk.

ે૭   ৬৪

SHAKER ROAST LEG OF LAMB

6 OR 7 POUND LEG OF LAMB
2 TABLESPOONS SWEET BUTTER
8 SHORT STALKS FRESHLY CUT ROSEMARY
1/2 TEASPOON SALT
1/8 TEASPOON PEPPER
1 TABLESPOON FLOUR

Wipe meat well and trim off all excess fat. Place in baking pan and cut shallow slices across leg. Melt butter and when hot dip the bunch of freshly cut rosemary in and lave the meat thoroughly with it. Then sprinkle meat with salt and pepper and dredge lightly with flour. Roast in a slow oven (250°) for 3 hours, basting frequently. If fresh rosemary is not at hand, mince fine 1/2 teaspoon of the dried herb, mix with heated butter and rub into roast. Serve with mashed parsnips. Serves 8-10.   Amelia's Shaker Recipes

ે૭   ৬৪

The Shakers thoroughly understood the use of herbs in the cooking of meats, salads and bland vegetables. Herbs to the Shakers "became an everyday necessity. The use of them simplified their menu, for it made of each dish a fascinating, outstanding viand." Meals were not planned by the wise Sisters merely to satisfy bodily hunger; primarily they must be nutritious but they must also "create contentment, joy and satisfaction to those who partake of them. . . ." What-ever the Shaker undertook to do, he or she put his whole

149

heart in the undertaking. In Shaker literature we constantly read that these devout religionists "had a passion for perfection." This by no means applies alone to their building furniture or weaving cloth—the Sisters in the great kitchens concocting breads and puddings were inspired with the very same zeal, to do the task at hand to the very best of their ability! "Do all your work as if you had a thousand years to live, and yet as you would if you knew you were to die tomorrow," was the rule Mother Ann left behind in kitchen, workshop, field and mill.

SISTER CLYMENA'S CHICKEN PIE

2 SMALL CHICKENS, ABOUT 3 POUNDS EACH
3 EGGS
1 PINT CREAM
1/2 SMALL ONION
4 SPRIGS PARSLEY, MINCED
4 SPRIGS CHERVIL, MINCED
SALT AND PEPPER TO TASTE
2 PASTRY CRUSTS (SEE INDEX)

Cut chickens in quarters; boil, well covered, in 2 cups of water for 30 minutes. Remove meat from bones, but leave in large pieces. Beat the eggs well and add cream, herbs and seasoning. Add enough of the hot chicken liquor to cream and eggs in order to cover chicken. Butter a baking dish well and line bottom and sides with your best biscuit dough. Fill with chicken mixture. Cover with top crust, allowing small vents for steam. Bake in hot oven (425°) for half an hour. Serve immediately with greens and a crisp salad. Serves 4-6.

North Union

Salt pork had great keeping quality. Beef was scarce in the early days in our land, and mutton, lamb and veal were extremely hard to preserve. Fresh meats were had only at slaughtering time among the early settlers in the rural districts.

"They shall be abundantly satisfied with the fatness of Thy house." Psalm 36.

BACHA BRINE

1 3/4 POUND SUGAR

2 POUNDS ROCK SALT

1 3/4 POUND SALTPETER

7 QUARTS HOT WATER

2 SHANKS OF BEEF, CUT FROM BETWEEN
   THE ROUND AND THE HOCK

Dissolve sugar, rock salt and saltpeter in hot water. When cool, pour over meat and let set for several weeks. This is sliced and pan broiled and is a delicious, tender meat.

The origin of the name is unknown. The recipe came from a manuscript cook book by Sister Lavina Clifford, of Canterbury Shakers, dated 1855. This was still a favorite dish at Canterbury when Sister Marguerite Forst was a girl.

Sister Marguerite, Canterbury

In collecting articles for a "Some-Time Shaker Museum" in Shaker Heights, Ohio, the primitive wooden sausage gun, the tremendous chopping bowls and the heavy chopping knives intrigued me especially. What volumes could be written on the devotion and endless thrift of the good Sisters

who wielded these clumsy utensils! The motto, "Give your
hands to work and your hearts to God," has a special meaning when we picture these patient, devout souls consecrated
to the act of preserving the meat supply for the great household committed to their care! In a time-yellowed kitchen
diary of North Union we read: "Packed fresh supply of meat
today; 7 barrels of salt pork and many firkins of sausage ready
for the storehouse. I did not weary, for I thought of tonight's
meeting constantly. Would many bright angels attend? Am
I worthy of their administrations? . . ."

Meatless Dishes

During the ten-year interim of Shaker Spiritualism (1837-1847) a ban was placed on meat eating by the Head Ministry at Mt. Lebanon. Meat had become almost the chief item of diet in this new land; often three, four or even more kinds were served at a single dinner, while fruits, vegetables, cereals and milk products were sadly neglected in the average diet. The "basic seven" so essential in our diet of today were wholly unknown!

In 1830 Fredrick Evans on visiting the Shakers found "them eminently sensible, candid and open minded." He

153

soon became one of their ranks. In *Shakerism*, by Anna White, we read: "Elder Fredrick's faith was not learned from priest nor from book but, like other prophets, from direct spiritual illumination. . . . This Shaker leader from 1836 to 1892 always stood on a mountain top calling aloud to his people 'To Come Up Higher!' " Elder Fredrick became a staunch vegetarian chiefly on humanitarian grounds and from the command—"Thou shalt not kill!" He claimed that if the slaughtering of animals was left completely to the consumers of their flesh, there would be very few meat eaters indeed! "Why make a graveyard of your stomach, when there are so many other good, wholesome things to eat?" was his reasoning. This great leader had a marked influence in bringing about a much more extensive use of whole grain, fresh fruits, green and leafy vegetables and milk products in not only the Shaker diet but also among "the World People" of his day. He was a prolific writer and lecturer; his numerous articles on diet appeared not only in the Shaker magazine, the *Manifesto*, but also in many important periodicals of his day. Many were the responses to his writing, from as far away as Switzerland, Germany, Scotland and England. Thrice he traveled to the British Isles and delivered lectures on better diets and hygiene as well as on universal peace and brotherly love.

In 1834 Daniel Frazer, another man endowed with a vigorous intellect, joined the Shaker ranks. Dietetics and hygiene were his special interests; he was a practical chemist and consequently was of great service to Shakerism in the days when the vegetarian philosophy, of which both he and Elder Fredrick were ardent adherents, was being established on a practical basis. Elder Daniel worked especially upon the value of milk and its products in diet, which today modern scientists declare to be an almost "complete food." Several of the Shakers were willing to prove Elder Daniel's theories about the great value of milk as a food, and for a year went on a "milk diet." Elder Daniel Offord, one of the most skilled mechanics and inventors among the Mt. Lebanon Shakers, lived on this diet with excellent results. All three of these reformers were strict vegetarians who maintained good health and lived to enjoy the rich fruits of old age.

Although Elder Fredrick looked forward to a day when all peoples would be vegetarians, the ban on meat eating was never strictly enforced throughout Shakerdom; it was left to the discretion of each member to decide for himself. However, in 1848 a strict ban was placed on pork as a food. This taboo was partly religious and partly for health reasons. Pork can be a dangerous menace to health, for it is often infected with parasites such as trichinae and tapeworm, which if not destroyed by sufficient heat in cooking will thrive in the consumer's body. Then, too, at that time hogs lived chiefly by consuming offal from the streets—they were the garbage collectors, the scavengers, and naturally were looked upon by the neat, sanitary Shakers as unclean creatures. This ban was finally lifted in the late 1870's, when the dairy industry became the chief occupation in many of the Shaker communities. The rule henceforth allowed "a sow for every cow" on the vast farms, in order to use up the whey and eliminate other waste.

Elder Fredrick Evans' motto: "It is good neither to eat flesh nor to drink wine nor anything whereby thy brother stumbleth or is offended." Romans 14:13. Like Paul, the great and generous-hearted Elder Fredrick was determined not to put a stumbling block in any fellow creature's way.

MUSHROOMS AND CHESTNUTS

1 POUND CHESTNUTS, SHELLED

2 TABLESPOONS BUTTER

1 POUND MUSHROOMS, QUARTERED

2 TABLESPOONS FLOUR

1 1/2 CUPS LIGHT CREAM

1/2 TEASPOON SALT

1/8 TEASPOON PEPPER

1 TABLESPOON PARSLEY, CHOPPED

Prick shells and place chestnuts in cold water and boil 15 minutes. Drain and remove shells and skin. Heat butter in skillet and cook quartered mushrooms until lightly browned. Blend in flour; slowly add cream and seasoning. Add nuts, cut in quarters. Heat thoroughly and garnish with chopped parsley. Serve with hot pone (see Index, Corn Bread) or with hot baked potatoes. Serves 3-4.

Amelia's Shaker Recipes

During the lengthy Shaker ban on pork, lard and all pork-drippings were relegated to soap-making, while beef suet and butter were rendered for deep-fat frying and for making pies. Butter was almost a "drug on the market" among the Shakers before wide markets were opened to them through better transportation. The Shakers had always used butter with a lavish hand; now they learned to render it— boil it in water and when cold remove the pure fat which rose to the top. Beef suet underwent this same process and was extensively used in making pies and pastries. Later, "cottalene," a combination of beef suet and cotton-seed oil, was commercially manufactured and put on the market, and was used by the skilled Shaker cooks in place of lard.

It is interesting to note that many of these "rendered

fats" were whipped or beaten (homogenized) until creamy before used in making pies. Chicken fat was treated in the same manner for pastry for chicken-pies. This made a delicious crust.

NUT AND RICE PATTIES

1 CUP CHESTNUTS, CHOPPED

1/2 CUP TOASTED BREAD CRUMBS

2 CUPS BOILED RICE

2 EGGS

1 TEASPOON PARSLEY, CHOPPED

2 TABLESPOONS RICH MILK

AN EXTRA EGG FOR DIPPING

Mix all ingredients well and shape into patties. Dip into beaten egg and dust with flour and fry to a rich brown. This is a very toothsome dish. Serves 4.   Union Village

During the meatless era, the Shaker Sisters never set before their hungry households dishes imitating or suggesting meat dishes, such as "mock duck" or "meatless meat loaf." They were always honest and straightforward in their cooking as in all their other dealings; nothing they made was ever camouflaged or dressed up to represent something different from what it was. It is said that in the fifteenth century in Europe a cook's chief ambition was to create dishes which could not be identified until eaten—that "often a turnip was dressed to look like a sardine or an ordinary meat-pie was dressed to resemble a peacock." The Shakers never adulterated or misrepresented their food or other works of their hands in any way. To them the Commandment "Thou shalt not lie or bear false witness" was just as vital to the better life as not committing murder or stealing.

This does not mean that the Shaker cooks were not heedful of eye-appeal in the preparation of their countless dishes! The wise Sisters well knew the value of contrasting color in foods, garnishes and neatly "dished" viands in whetting appetites.

Chestnuts were most plentiful on the Heights where the Shakers dwelt, as were black walnuts and hickory nuts. All three of these tasty nuts added their rich flavor to many a Shaker dish, especially during the meatless era of Shakerdom.

SHAKER BAKED BEANS

4 CUPS NAVY BEANS
2 1/2 CUPS HOT WATER
1 ONION
1/2 CUP MOLASSES
1/2 CUP BUTTER
1 TEASPOON SALT
2 TEASPOONS DRY MUSTARD
1/2 CUP TOMATO CATSUP

Soak the beans overnight. Drain and cook in fresh water until tender. Peel onion and place in bottom of well-buttered bean pot. Drain beans and save liquid. Pour beans into bean pot. Add molasses, butter, salt, dry mustard and catsup to bean liquid and pour over beans. Cover pot and cook in very slow oven for 3 hours. Add more liquid whenever necessary. Remove cover for last half hour and brown well. Serves 10-12.   Sister Josephine, Canterbury

This excellent recipe for baked beans was used during the Shaker ban on pork. Several older Shaker "receipts" for this dish call for "medium thick slices of salt pork laid in the bottom of the bean pot which gradually work their way to the top and flavor the entire contents of the pot as they rise to the surface!" When salt pork was used, the butter was omitted.

Even in recent years the sisters at Canterbury in New Hampshire sent dozens of pots of hot baked beans every Friday to regular customers in the vicinity. Now they are selling the empty pots to eager collectors of Shaker items. These sturdy, wide-mouthed pots, which have so amply served the Shakers for over a hundred years of good cooking, were made at Bennington and are worthy reminders of pioneer days in this fair land of ours.

CHESTNUT OMELET

4 EGGS, SEPARATED

1/2 TEASPOON SALT

1 TABLESPOON SUGAR

1 CUP LIGHT CREAM

2 CUPS FLOUR

1/2 TEASPOONS BAKING POWDER

2 CUPS CHESTNUTS, BOILED AND CHOPPED

Beat egg yolks and add salt, sugar and cream. Stir in flour until smooth. Fold in the stiffly beaten egg whites to which the baking powder had been added. Add chestnuts and turn into a hot buttered skillet. Cook until lightly browned on bottom. Place in (350°) oven until top is dry to the touch. Serves 4 amply.   Amelia's Shaker Recipes

Not a single nut went to waste on the large Shaker estates. Chestnuts were very plentiful in the early days and were used by the Shakers in many ways—in stuffings, plain roasted and made in sundry combinations with eggs, rice and mushrooms. After the first frost in the autumn, the Shaker children were up before dawn to gather the precious harvest before the squirrels garnered them. After drying them in their attics, the hickory, butter and walnuts were cracked by the children. Quantities of them were consumed as a treat at Christmas time while other great quantities were fashioned into cakes, candies and cookies.

SHAKER RAREBIT

1/2 POUND YANKEE CHEESE
1 PINT MILK
1/2 TEASPOON SALT
DASH OF RED PEPPER

Chop cheese and add to milk. Let come to a slow boil and stir until very smooth. Add seasoning and pour over rounds of hot buttered toast. Serves 4.

Or

1/2 POUND SWISS CHEESE
3/4 CUP CIDER
1/2 TEASPOON SALT
TOASTED BREAD

Slice cheese fine. Lay in a baking dish and cover with cider. Let set for 4 hours. Place over a low heat and stir until smooth. Pour over piping hot toast and serve at once. Serves 4.   Pleasant Hill, Kentucky

During the Shaker ban on meat, cheese soufflés, noodles baked with cheese, rarebits and just sliced cheese took the place of meat at the great Shaker tables where fifty Brethren ate on one side of the dining halls while fifty thrifty Sisters occupied the table on the other side. The Shakers were skilled cheese-makers. The problem of marketing the milk of their large herds led to their making vast amounts of cheese. After the milk had coagulated into curd, it was heated and gradually separated from the liquid or whey. The curd was then salted and left to ripen, with the aid of necessary bacteria which helped to break down the protein into a more digestible form. The taste and kind of cheese made depended upon the treatment and storage. The great cheese-presses which broke up the ripening curd were worked by the Shaker Brethren. The whey-bleached cheese baskets and a few remaining recipes are all that are left to tell the story of this once-thriving Shaker industry.

LENTIL LOAF

2 CUPS DRIED LENTILS, COOKED

1/4 POUND AMERICAN CHEESE

1 CUP SOFT BREAD CRUMBS,

1 TABLESPOON ONION, GRATED

1 TEASPOON SALT

1/8 TEASPOON PEPPER

4 TABLESPOONS SOFT BUTTER

Pass parboiled lentils and cheese through food grinder. Add other ingredients and shape into loaf. Bake 45 minutes at 350°, basting often with butter and a few drops of water. Serves 6. Serve with Tasty Tomato Sauce (see below).

South Union

TASTY TOMATO SAUCE

3 TABLESPOONS BUTTER
1 CLOVE GARLIC, WHOLE
1 LARGE ONION, MINCED
1 QUART COOKED TOMATOES, STRAINED
8 SPRIGS PARSLEY
1 SPRIG THYME
4 CELERY TOPS
SALT AND PEPPER
1 TEASPOON SUGAR

Heat butter and drop garlic in for 2 minutes. Remove garlic and add minced onion; stir until light brown. Add strained tomatoes and drop into this the parsley, thyme and celery tops tied together. Season with salt and pepper and bring to a boil. Reduce heat and simmer for 20 minutes, stirring frequently. Remove herbs and add sugar. Serve hot.

MUSHROOM SAUCE

2 CUPS MUSHROOMS, SLICED
3 TABLESPOONS BUTTER
2 TABLESPOONS FLOUR
2 CUPS RICH MILK
SALT AND PEPPER
1 TEASPOON PARSLEY, MINCED

Sauté mushrooms in butter; when slightly browned, blend in flour and stir well. When flour is slightly browned, gradually add milk and blend until smooth. Add salt, pepper and parsley. Serve hot.

162

SHAKER DOLMAS

2 QUARTS GRAPE LEAVES, BLANCHED

1 CUP RICE, UNCOOKED

1/2 CUP ONIONS, CHOPPED

2 TABLESPOONS SOFT BUTTER

1/8 TEASPOON THYME, MINCED

1/2 TEASPOON SALT

1/4 TEASPOON PEPPER

1/2 TEASPOON PARSLEY, MINCED

2 CUPS STOCK

Place the blanched grape leaves on a board. Mix all ingredients and put a tablespoonful on each leaf; roll each leaf and tuck in edges. Make a nest of grape leaves in bottom of kettle. Put in dolmas and cover with rest of leaves. Weight down with inverted plate. Pour on 2 cups of boiling stock. Boil slowly until all liquid is absorbed by rice. Serve very hot. Serves 6.

It is not known how this dish, which came from the Near East, got into Shaker cookery, but due to the fact that they cultivated the vine and used its leaves in pickling, they probably learned to appreciate the tasty quality of the grape leaf and soon were enjoying dolmas.

SHAKER CHEESE BALLS

Take a crock full of clabber and set it back on the stove to ripen and separate. When set, pour into a cheese basket lined with fresh cheesecloth and drip until dry. Season with salt, white pepper, butter and rich cream. Mold into small balls and roll in chopped chives. Chill and serve with dark rye bread. Amelia's Shaker Recipes

The Shakers made a large variety of cheese ranging from cottage cheese, cream cheese, a solid Yankee cheese type to a rich, mellow variety resembling Swiss cheese besides several fine herb-laden varieties which are still remembered by some early settlers of Shaker Heights as delicious and flavorful.

Today we know that cheese is a valuable food; that it is the congealed protein of milk plus some fats; that it is rich in vitamin A and some valuable minerals. It is a rich, pleasing and digestible food.

CHEESE OMELET

6 SLICES BREAD, WELL BUTTERED
1/4 TEASPOON PREPARED MUSTARD
1 POUND YANKEE CHEESE
4 EGGS
2 CUPS MILK
1/2 TEASPOON SALT
1/4 TEASPOON PEPPER

Butter a baking dish; cover the bottom with medium-thick slices of bread well buttered and lightly spread with prepared mustard. Then cover lavishly with thin slices of cheese. Repeat the layer. Pour the well-beaten eggs over this and add milk; season. Bake for 30 minutes in a moderate (350°) oven. Serve very hot. Serves 4.

Sister Mary, Enfield Shakers

SHAKER CHEESE SOUFFLÉ

2 TABLESPOONS BUTTER

2 TABLESPOONS FLOUR

1 CUP MILK

1/2 TEASPOON SALT

1/4 TEASPOON PEPPER

DASH CAYENNE PEPPER

1 CUP SHARP CHEESE, SHAVED

3 EGGS, SEPARATED

Melt butter over low flame, add flour and blend well; add milk and stir to perfect smoothness. Season. Stir in shaved cheese and stir until blended. Then add egg yolks slightly beaten. Set aside to cool. Beat whites very stiff and fold into mixture. Pour into a buttered baking dish and set dish in a pan of hot water. Bake 35 minutes in a slow oven (325°). Serves 3-4.   Sister Abigail

Eggs and cheese were called "white meat" during the Middle Ages and were extensively used by the people of Europe, for game and meat were often exclusively the property of the king and nobles. Shooting a hare in the King's forest was often punished by chopping off the hunter's ears! With the expansion of commerce and travel, butter and cheese-making became thriving industries throughout Europe.

By 1850 it was found that the clay soil at North Union Shaker community was better adapted to raising herds than grain. Their deep cellars and cold spring-houses were soon richly stocked with ripening cheeses of varied sorts.

Eldress Anna White of Mt. Lebanon was a great believer in "the bloodless diet; the vegetarians had their special table at this community, but in time the whole family united and found as the years passed that the abundant diet of grains, vegetables, fruits, eggs and milk products has answered every physiological need as well as satisfying the conscience of the consumer."

Pies & Pastries

The North Union founders, having come from New England, brought with them the skill of pie-making. After the grist mill began grinding an ample assortment of flours and meals, the Shaker Sisters showed great ingenuity in wrapping most anything edible—from garden, herd, flock and orchard—in an endless variety of pastries. The Brethren, coming in to breakfast at six o'clock after an hour or more of milking and other heavy chores, wanted something solid and satisfying—something that would "stick to the ribs," such as hash, eggs, oatmeal, stewed fruits, an ample slice of coffee cake, a slab of pie or several doughnuts. In the Shaker pantries there was a constant rotation of green and dried apple pies, and when the apple-bins had to be scraped in the late winter for the last few greenings and wine-saps, delicate custards were added to stretch out this favorite fare. All summer there were berries and other lush fruits, both wild and cultivated, which the skillful Sisters encased in crusty pastry. Then, later, cranberries, mincemeat, squash and pumpkin filled the shells. The Shakers had a veritable calendar of pies!

From New England the Shaker Sisters brought with them the terms trap, coffin, grated and tart pie. The trap was a deep-dish pie often of meat, fowl or fruit. When this trap was covered with a top crust it was called a coffin, for it was baked in a loaf pan and resembled a coffer or coffin. When the tart was latticed over with narrow strips of pastry it was termed a grated pie, while the shallow, open fruit pie was called a tart.

Again there were sundry pastries for the various foods: "Venison and mutton must be baked in a moist, thick and lasting crust for which a rye-paste is the best. Turkey, veal and lamb should be baked in a good white flour crust, somewhat thick. Chicken, quince and mincemeat, which must be eaten hot, should have the finest, shortest wheaten crust. . . . For tarts use puff-paste made from the choicest wheaten flour and butter. This must be handled gently . . ." the old annals record.

The same butter- and time-stained records state: "To a gallon of flour take a pound of the best butter boiled in a little pure water and make up the paste as quickly and lightly as possible. . . ." Or: "Take a gallon of wheat flour, a pound of sugar, half a pound of butter, a pinch of saffron [it gives it a lush look]; work this up with three eggs beaten to a froth, with cinnamon and a cup of rosewater."

During the Shaker ban on pork, beef suet was rendered

and used for shortening in pie and pastry making. It was chopped, put in a large iron pot, covered with warm water and simmered until suet was melted. After straining, when cold the fat would harden on top of water. This was beaten until fluffy and used.

PASTRY

2 1/4 CUPS FLOUR, SIFTED
1/2 TEASPOON SALT
2/3 CUP SHORTENING, CHILLED
1/3 CUP COLD WATER

Sift flour with salt into mixing bowl. Cut in the shortening with pastry blender until the particles are the size of a pea. Add water very gradually by sprinkling it in. Do not get the crumbs too fine and beware of getting dough too wet. Handle the dough as little as possible. Form lightly into 2 balls and chill. Roll out on a lightly floured board to 1/8 inch thickness.   North Union

SISTER LETTIE'S BUTTER PASTRY

2 1/4 CUPS FLOUR, SIFTED
1/2 TEASPOON SALT
1/2 TEASPOON BAKING POWDER
2/3 CUP UNSALTED BUTTER, CHILLED
1/3 CUP COLD WATER

The most important point in making a flaky crust is to have the shortening well chilled. This keeps the crumbs from getting too fine. It is best to use a blender, or two knives, in cutting in the shortening, for if done with fingers, the warmth of the hand softens shortening and makes dough tough. Form into 2 balls; chill slightly and roll to 1/8 inch thickness. This crust is especially suited to berry pies.

 है•   ৶§

SISTER LOTTIE'S NUT CRUST

2/3 CUP GRAHAM CRACKER CRUMBS
2/3 CUP WALNUT MEATS, CHOPPED
1/8 CUP BUTTER, MELTED
1 EGG WHITE, UNBEATEN

Mix crumbs and chopped nut meats. (The original recipe calls for black walnuts, which are not easily obtained today.) Work in the melted butter and the unbeaten egg white and press into the bottom and sides of a 9-inch pie plate. Bake in moderate (350°) oven 8 to 10 minutes. Cool before adding cream or custard filling.

 है•   ৶§

Among the North Union Household Hints we read: "For flakier pie crust, beat the lard until it is light and fluffy before using." Today we know homogenized fats make better crusts.

 है•   ৶§

SHAKER APPLE PIE

3 CUPS SOUR APPLES, PEELED AND SLICED
2/3 CUP SUGAR, EITHER MAPLE OR WHITE
1 TABLESPOON CREAM
1 TABLESPOON ROSEWATER (SEE INDEX)

PASTRY FOR 2 NINE-INCH CRUSTS (SEE ABOVE)

Slice apples into mixing bowl and add sugar, cream and rosewater and mix thoroughly so that rosewater will be distributed evenly. Line the pie dish with favorite pastry; fill with the apple mixture and cover with top crust in which a few small vents have been slashed for steam to escape. Flute the edges well to keep juice from escaping. Brush over with a very little rosewater mixed with milk. Bake in a moderate oven (350°) for 50 minutes.

Old Canterbury

KENTUCKY SHOO FLY PIE

3/4 CUP DARK MOLASSES
3/4 CUP VERY HOT WATER
1/2 TEASPOON SODA
1 1/2 CUPS FLOUR
1/2 CUP SUGAR, BROWN OR MAPLE
1/4 CUP BUTTER
PASTRY FOR 1 CRUST (SEE ABOVE)

Mix molasses with hot water and blend well. Blend flour, sugar and soda and cut in butter to a coarse crumb. Line pie dish with pastry. Pour in 1/3 of molasses mixture and top with 1/3 crumb mixture. Repeat adding alternate layers with crumb on top. Bake for about 35 minutes at 375°.

South Union

MINCEMEAT FOR PIES

3 POUND BEEF TONGUE, BOILED AND
  CHOPPED FINE
1/2 POUND SUET, CHOPPED FINE
2 POUNDS SEEDED RAISINS
2 POUNDS CURRANTS
2 POUNDS SUGAR, WHITE
2 POUNDS SUGAR, DARK BROWN
1/2 POUND CITRON, CUT FINE
1/4 POUND CANDIED ORANGE PEEL, CUT FINE
3 PINTS SOUR APPLES, CHOPPED
1 TABLESPOON CINNAMON
1 NUTMEG, GRATED
1 TEASPOON ALLSPICE
1/2 TEASPOON SALT
RIND AND JUICE OF 2 LEMONS
1 CUP BOILED-DOWN CIDER
1/2 CUP BRANDY

Blend all ingredients well and put into large crock to ripen. The boiled-down cider and touch of brandy will keep it from spoiling while ripening. Keep sealed for at least 4 weeks in a cool place before using in pies. Bake between 2 crusts and serve hot. Old Enfield

Mince pies were baked by the dozen by the Shakers and stored in barrels in some cold place where they froze and kept perfectly until used, when they were thawed out, then heated and eaten good and hot with lemon sauce.

SHAKER LEMON PIE

2 LEMONS
4 TABLESPOONS CORNSTARCH

1 1/4 CUPS SUGAR

3 EGG YOLKS, BEATEN

2 CUPS BOILING WATER

3 EGG WHITES

1/8 TEASPOON SALT

2 TABLESPOONS SUGAR

1/2 TABLESPOON LEMON JUICE

1 BAKED PIE SHELL (SEE BEGINNING OF CHAPTER)

Roll lemons thoroughly; grate off the yellow rind and keep. Squeeze out juice. Make a boiled custard of cornstarch, sugar, beaten egg yolks and water. Add rind and juice of lemons. Stir until smooth and turn into baked pie shell. Beat egg whites with salt; when stiff gradually add sugar and 1/2 tablespoon lemon juice. Top custard with meringue and bake in slow oven until well browned.

Union Village

OHIO LEMON PIE

2 LEMONS

2 CUPS SUGAR

PASTRY FOR 2 CRUSTS (SEE BEGINNING OF CHAPTER)

4 EGGS

This is yet another very old lemon pie recipe which the early Ohio Shakers fashioned frequently. "Slice two lemons as thin as paper, rind and all. Place them in a bowl [it states, yellow bowl] and pour over them 2 cups of sugar. Mix well and let stand for 2 hours or better. Then go about making your best pastry for 2 crusts. Line a pie dish with same. Beat 4 eggs together and pour over lemons. Fill unbaked pieshell with this and add top crust with small vents cut to let out steam. Place in a hot oven at 450° for 15 minutes and then cut down heat and bake until a silver knife inserted into custard comes out clean."

RHUBARB OR PIEPLANT PIE

2 CUPS PIEPLANT, CUT IN INCH PIECES

1 1/2 CUPS BROWN SUGAR

1 TABLESPOON FLOUR

3 TABLESPOONS BUTTER

PASTRY FOR 2 CRUSTS (SEE BEGINNING OF CHAPTER)

Combine pieplant with sugar and flour, and turn into un-baked shell. Dot well with butter, for the butter reduces the acid and takes the place of extra sugar. Cover with top crust, allowing steam vents, and bake in hot (450°) oven for 15 minutes; lessen heat and bake until well browned.

North Union

Always pull pieplant when young instead of cutting it. Use as soon as possible after pulling, for it loses sugar. Much of the true flavor as well as the color is in the skin, so do not peel unless tough. For sauce, cut in 2 inch lengths; cover generously with sugar and let stand for 2 hours. Boil only five minutes in its own juice—never add water. If you are short of sugar, substitute butter for sugar in making sauce.

SISTER LETTIE'S MAPLE PIE

2 TABLESPOONS BUTTER

1 CUP MAPLE SUGAR

1 1/4 CUPS HOT MILK

3 EGGS

2 TABLESPOONS CORNSTARCH

1/8 CUP COLD MILK

1/2 TEASPOON SALT

1 UNBAKED PASTRY SHELL (SEE BEGINNING OF
   CHAPTER)
1/8 TEASPOON NUTMEG

Melt butter and blend in maple sugar; gradually add hot milk and stir until sugar is well dissolved. Beat eggs, wet cornstarch with cold milk and blend with hot mixture. Add salt. Turn into unbaked pie shell and sprinkle with nutmeg. Bake in a moderate (350°) oven until custard is set, or until a silver knife inserted into it comes out clean.

Many of the early Shaker recipes call for maple sugar, maple syrup, honey, molasses or sorghum instead of white sugar, which was very scarce in the pioneer days at the frontier. Today the reverse is true. Maple sugar and syrup are becoming very scarce due to the fact that more than 93% of our native forests have been cleared. Even today there is a great demand for maple timber, which is converted into cottage furniture and into the manufacturing of heels for women's shoes.

SHAKER CRANBERRY PIE

3/4 CUP SUGAR
1 TABLESPOON FLOUR
1 TEASPOON VANILLA
1 CUP RAISINS
1 CUP CRANBERRIES
PASTRY FOR 2 CRUSTS (SEE BEGINNING OF
   CHAPTER)

Mix sugar with flour and vanilla; sprinkle over fruit and mix well. Bake between two pie crusts. This is a very tasty confection.

This is an old Shaker recipe taken from the Harvard Woman's Club Cook Book, compiled in 1916. The same recipe is in my mother's Shaker gleanings on good cookery.

SHAKER CIDER PIE

1/2 CUP BOILED-DOWN CIDER
1 TABLESPOON BUTTER
1 CUP MAPLE SUGAR
1/4 CUP WATER
DASH OF SALT
2 EGG YOLKS, BEATEN
2 EGG WHITES, BEATEN
1 UNBAKED PIE SHELL (SEE BEGINNING OF CHAPTER)
DASH OF NUTMEG

Boil down cider until it is a rich, dark syrup. Take 1/2 cup of this and put in saucepan; add butter, sugar, water and a dash of salt, and simmer several minutes. Cool slightly. and add beaten egg yolks; now fold in stiffly beaten egg whites. Pour into unbaked shell. Dust with nutmeg and bake until shell is brown and custard well set.

South Union

The cider used should be the old-fashioned boiled-down Shaker cider—"thick, dark and tangy." The Shakers boiled down great quantities of this rich beverage each fall, which served many purposes during the year. Nor was Shaker cider made from spoiled, discarded fruit! Certain kinds of apples, especially juicy and flavorful, were gathered for cider and placed in a cool place in the shade of their great barns to mellow. On a certain fall day when the perfume of this juicy horde became pungent, into the greedy cider presses they were fed and converted into amber liquid. This was allowed to ripen for several days but not to "harden." No preservative was ever used—except boiling it down and bottling it.

ह•   •ई

PUMPKIN PIE

1 CUP PUMPKIN, COOKED AND STRAINED
2/3 CUP SUGAR, MAPLE OR BROWN
1/2 TEASPOON GINGER
1/2 TEASPOON CINNAMON
3 EGGS
2 CUPS RICH MILK
1/2 TEASPOON SALT
1 UNBAKED PIE SHELL (SEE BEGINNING OF
    CHAPTER)

Mix all ingredients together; blend thoroughly. Pour into unbaked pie shell and bake in moderate (350°) oven until inserted knife blade comes out clean.

Amelia's Shaker Recipes

ह•   •ई

The first pumpkin baked at this frontier was made without flaky pie crust. The recipe reads: "Cut out the stem end from a pumpkin and save; scoop out seeds and loose fiber. Fill two-thirds full of milk sweetened with maple sugar or syrup (or honey will do as well) and add whatever spices you have on hand. Put lid back on and place in (brick) oven for five or six hours. Put on table and scoop out and serve with butter and molasses. It makes a good dessert."

Both winter squash and carrots were substituted if the supply of pumpkins gave out.

"One secret of good pumpkin pie is to include at least 1/2 teaspoon of ground ginger among the spices. . . . Pompion, as the Pilgrim Fathers called the pumpkin, was the fruit which the Lord was pleased to feed his people till corn and cattle found increase."—From the Governor's Journal.

SISTER LIZZIE'S SUGAR PIE

1 DEEP UNBAKED PIE SHELL (SEE BEGINNING OF
   CHAPTER)
1/2 CUP SOFT BUTTER
1 CUP SUGAR, MAPLE OR BROWN
   (WHITE CAN BE USED)
1/4 CUP FLOUR, SIFTED
2 CUPS CREAM
1/2 TEASPOON VANILLA OR ROSEWATER
1/8 TEASPOON NUTMEG

Line a deep pie dish with your best pastry. Cream butter and spread over bottom. Then sprinkle with sugar. Repeat this process and sprinkle last layer with flour. Flavor the cream with vanilla or with rosewater and pour over pie. Dust with nutmeg. Bake in hot oven (450°) for 10 minutes. Reduce heat to 350° and bake until a knife blade inserted in the pie comes out clean. This is a toothsome pie, especially beloved by children and a good recipe to fall back on when the apple-bins are empty in the spring.

South Union

At the Canterbury Shaker community there is a huge pie oven with rotating racks which once held sixty golden-crusted pies. And such pies! This was a very clever and ingenious arrangement, for the heat was thus evenly distributed and the baked pies were removed from the oven with no difficulty whatever.

Pickles

On reading the hand-written annals on Shaker food, it seems these thrifty Sisters pickled or preserved most anything, from the first tiny cucumber and pale shallot to the late seckel pear and the last frost-bitten green tomato. Enormous crocks were filled with "Pickled Lily"—a combination of various chopped vegetables, spices and vinegars. Others contained stuffed peppers or mangoes for which there was a tremendous demand in February and March in the Cleveland markets. Translucent watermelon rind, lush spiced peaches and delicious little red crab apples steeped in their richly seasoned juices filled innumerable crocks in the great deep cellars of the Shakers. Not a bean or a gooseberry went to waste on these vast Shaker farms where from two to six families, ranging from 30 to 100 persons, were served three square meals daily for 365 days of the year. Then, too, there were many wayfarers who sought food at these hospitable gates and many visiting Ministries from the other Shaker communities, who often sojourned for several weeks at a time.

The Sisters, preparing the food for these large households, realized how these condiments and pickles "dressed up simple fare and added needed variety to their limited winter and spring diet." Moreover, vinegar was the great preservative of food in the days before refrigeration. The Shakers lived chiefly on what they raised. What was not immediately consumed by the large household must of necessity be salvaged for the long winter and early spring ahead! Sugar was mighty scarce among them in the old days; maple and honey were the sweetening agents. Containers also were at a terrible premium; therefore drying and pickling were necessary. They made their own wooden containers: firkins, runlets, keelers, kegs and barrels in their cooper shop, and earthen crocks were purchased from the nearest pottery.

Again, the history of food reveals that man craved and sought after condiments, salt, vinegars, spices and onions as far back as records extend. These are the substances which add relish and interest to food. Man's insatiable desire for these palate pleasers, especially spices, has added volumes of romance, adventure and even warfare to the history of mankind! The history of our favorite spices is the story of the rise and fall of great empires!

The hunger for salt among man and most beasts has been universal. Cinnamon, ginger, cloves, nutmeg and pepper, all native to the spice islands about India and China, have been used by man since earliest times. These were not always used as flavorings of food; at first they were used for medicinal purposes, and were also offered as incense upon altars. Thus they gained their fantastic glamor. During the Middle Ages pepper became the queen of all spices and was so universally prized "that it could function as money anywhere."

True pepper is the berry of a fruit on a catkin which originally grew on the Malabar coast. So anxious was Columbus to discover "the priceless spice islands," that when he discovered the American continent, he found a tree with spicy berries (allspice) which he named pepper. Later, in Central America, he discovered a spicy fruit (our red and green peppers) which led him to believe that he had actually found true pepper. Hence the misnomer.

Until recent times spices and spiced vinegars were considered an essential part of diet. Although we know today that these have no nutritive value, we still treasure them as whetters of appetite and as essential factors in adding variety to diet. Dietitians tell us that there is a certain "intangible psychological demand for foods which is as real to man as the need for vitamins and energy." This demand accounts for the following chapter on Shaker pickles!

CRISP PICKLES

Throw small cucumber pickles in a vat of brine strong enough "to float an egg." After a week pour off the brine and rinse pickles well. Place the pickles in large crocks and cover with the best vinegar; let stand for a couple of weeks longer. Then turn them into a brass cauldron with a goodly lump of alum and let them scald slowly over a very low heat. By no means let them come to a proper boil. They will now be a lovely green, and firm as well. Now add onions, horseradish, green and red peppers or anything that suits your taste. In packing away in crocks, scatter oak leaves among the layers and cover the top with these same leaves. This will prevent the pickles from softening.   North Union

"If you wish plump pickles, fill your large pickling kettle half full of small cucumbers (2 inches in length) , and then fill the kettle almost to the top with cold water. Put on the stove and heat almost to boiling point. Pour off the water immediately and refill with cold water. Do this nine times and you will not have wilted, shrunken pickles. If you wish crisp pickles, add a lump of alum to the last water. Spice your vinegar to suit your taste and pour on hot."—Eldress Clymena

The Shaker seed catalogue shows that they raised both cucumbers and pickles; the latter was a small, thin-skinned variety far different from the large cucumber, which the Shakers used raw for salad, or baked, stewed and stuffed.

WATERMELON RIND PICKLE

7 POUNDS WATERMELON RIND, PEELED

2 1/2 QUARTS WATER

1/3 CUP SALT

6 1/2 CUPS BROWN SUGAR

2 CUPS VINEGAR

1 CUP WATER

1 TABLESPOON CLOVES, WHOLE

2 STICKS CINNAMON

2 LEMONS

Pare off the outer green from watermelon rind and cut in inch squares. Put in large bowl and pour over them the salt and water mixed. Let soak for three days. Drain and let stand in fresh water for one hour. Make a syrup of sugar, vinegar, water and spices. Cut the lemon (rind and all) paper thin. Put melon and lemon into hot syrup and boil until watermelon is clear. Seal in jars.   South Union

SWEET PICKLED FRUIT

7 POUNDS FRUIT, EITHER CRAB APPLES, SECKEL PEARS
   OR SOLID PLUMS
7 CUPS SUGAR
2 QUARTS VINEGAR
4 STICKS CINNAMON
2 OUNCES CASSIA BUDS OR CLOVES

If crab apples or plums are used, wash but do not pare. If pears are preferred, pare but leave on stems. Combine sugar, vinegar and spices and boil 5 minutes. Add fruit and cook slowly until fruit is tender but not soft. Let stand in syrup overnight. Drain off syrup and cook until of honey consistency. Pack fruit in jars, cover with boiling syrup and seal at once. Mary Whitcher's *Shaker Housekeeper*

Cloves and nutmeg are two ancient spices that once were worth more than their weight in gold. They were symbols of great luxury, for only the very wealthy could afford to use them.

Nutmeg and mace have been used by Europeans since the twelfth century. They grow on the same plant; nutmeg is the fruit or berry and mace is the fibrous covering of the fruit.

SHAKER CUT PICKLES

4 QUARTS MEDIUM-SIZED CUCUMBERS, CUT IN CHUNKS
1/2 CUP SALT
BOILING WATER
3 CUPS VINEGAR

184

1 CUP WATER

2 CUPS SUGAR

1 TEASPOON DRY MUSTARD

1 TEASPOON ALLSPICE

1 TEASPOON CELERY SEED

1 TEASPOON MUSTARD SEED

1 TEASPOON TUMERIC

Wash and cut cucumbers, add salt and cover with boiling water; let stand overnight. Make a syrup of vinegar, water, sugar and spices. When syrup boils, drain pickles and add to hot mixture. Let come to a boil, pack into jars at once and seal.   South Union

PICKLED PEACHES

7 POUNDS RIPE CLING STONE PEACHES

1/4 CUP WHOLE CLOVES

1/4 CUP STICK CINNAMON, BROKEN

1/4 CUP WHOLE ALLSPICE

8 CUPS SUGAR

1 QUART VINEGAR

Wipe all the fuzz from peaches and insert 3 cloves in each. Put the remaining spices in a bag, add sugar and vinegar and boil 10 minutes. Pour while very hot over peaches. Do this three mornings in succession, heating syrup to boil each time. The fourth morning scald the fruit in the syrup, pack in earthen jars and seal.   Amelia's Shaker Recipes

PICKLED ONIONS

2 QUARTS VERY SMALL WHITE ONIONS
1 QUART MILK
1 QUART WATER
1 QUART VINEGAR
1 TABLESPOON SUGAR (OPTIONAL)
1/8 CUP GRATED HORSERADISH (OPTIONAL)

Divest very small white onions of their outer tunics and boil
in equal parts of milk and water. Pour off liquid when onions
are clear and pour on scalding vinegar. Horseradish and sugar
or spices may be added if desired. Very good as they are.

Sister Marguerite, Canterbury

PICKLED GRAPES

8 POUNDS HALF-RIPE GRAPES
4 POUNDS BROWN SUGAR
2 QUARTS WINE VINEGAR
1/2 CUP CLOVES, WHOLE
1/2 CUP ALLSPICE, WHOLE
1/2 CUP STICK CINNAMON, BROKEN

Do not use ripe grapes; a half-ripe catawba grape is most suitable. Pick grapes from the stem and place in jars. Make a
syrup of sugar, vinegar and spices tied in cloth. Or better yet
use 8 drops each of oil of cloves, allspice and cinnamon, for
this will give a very clear pickle. Pour syrup very hot over
grapes in jars and seal. This is excellent with ham or fowl.

Amelia's Shaker Recipes

PICKLED BELL PEPPERS

8 POUNDS BELL PEPPERS (SWEET GREEN PEPPERS)
1 CUP SALT
1 GALLON WATER
1 HEAD CABBAGE, CHOPPED
20 MEDIUM-SIZED ONIONS, CHOPPED
1 CUP FRESHLY GRATED HORSERADISH
1/2 CUP MUSTARD SEED
1/2 CUP CLOVES, POWDERED
VINEGAR

Wash peppers and cut off tops with sharp knife; remove seeds. Keep tops. Soak in brine overnight. Next morning chop fine the cabbage and onions, mix with grated horseradish, mustard seed and cloves. Stuff peppers and tie on tops with kitchen thread. Pack in earthen crocks with layers of grape leaves between. Cover with hot vinegar, and seal. These will be excellent late into the following spring and are considered a great appetizer. North Union

The North Union Sisters made literally hundreds of crocks of these pickled peppers, or pickled mangoes, for the financial records show that in late spring there was a great demand for them by the Cleveland housewife. "Sold 10 crocks of pickled mangoes" is a common entry in their household accounts.

In the early days the Shakers ground all their spices at home by means of spice mills. If mills were not available, they were ground in a metal mortar or bruised and crushed with a cleaver. Thus the greatest amount of goodness was obtained from these precious substances. "A nutmeg sweats oil when pricked with a needle; always prick them to see if they are fresh," the Shaker Sisters advise. Perhaps the real intention in pricking them was to see if they were carved or turned from wood such as some Yankee peddler once foisted off on his public!

ع&

SPICED VINEGAR

2 OUNCES WHOLE PEPPER, BRUISED
1 OUNCE GINGER, BRUISED
1 OUNCE ALLSPICE
1 OUNCE SALT

Mix all ingredients together; if a hotter flavor is desired, add one half dram cayenne. Add to 1 quart of vinegar and simmer until flavor is extracted. Pour over pickles.

GRAPE CATSUP

5 POUNDS GRAPES, STEMMED
2 POUNDS SUGAR, MAPLE OR BROWN
1 TABLESPOON CLOVES, GROUND
1 TABLESPOON CINNAMON
1 TABLESPOON PEPPER
1 TABLESPOON ALLSPICE
1 TEASPOON SALT
1 PINT OF BEST WINE VINEGAR

Pluck grapes from stems. Put in granite pot; cover and simmer 10 minutes. Pass through a sieve. Add spices, sugar and vinegar and boil gently until thickened. Pour into containers and seal. This is highly desirable for cold meats.

Amelia's Shaker Recipes

Like many of the Shaker communities, North Union had extensive vineyards. There were large packing and ware houses on the premises. The Lake Shore Railroad passed through this property. Tons of grapes were packed and shipped both east and west from these warehouses. Other great quantities were made into medicinal wines, barrels upon barrels of wine vinegar, grape juice, catsup, spiced grapes and the never-to-be-forgotten fall confection—Concord grape pie! Late varieties, such as catawbas, which withstood the light frosts and were harvested late, had their stems sealed with beeswax and were packed in sawdust to be used at Thanksgiving.

GOOSEBERRY CATSUP

8 CUPS GOOSEBERRIES

4 CUPS SUGAR

1 TEASPOON SALT

1 TABLESPOON CINNAMON, GROUND

1 TABLESPOON CLOVES, GROUND

1 TEASPOON PEPPER

1 CUP VINEGAR

With small scissors cut both stem and blossom ends from gooseberries. Mix spices and seasoning with vinegar and bring to boil. Add berries and cook until thick. Pour into jars and seal. Delicious with ham. Union Village

CORN RELISH

4 CUPS ONIONS, CHOPPED

4 CUPS RIPE TOMATOES

4 CUPS CUCUMBERS, CHOPPED

4 CUPS CORN, CUT FROM COB

4 CUPS CABBAGE, CHOPPED

4 CUPS SUGAR

1 TABLESPOON SALT

1 TABLESPOON CELERY SEED

1 TEASPOON TUMERIC

4 CUPS VINEGAR

Remove skins from onions and tomatoes and hard ends from cucumbers. Chop all vegetables and mix together. Combine sugar, salt and spices with vinegar; add vegetables and cook 20 minutes. Put into jars and seal.　　　　North Union

CRANBERRY RELISH

2 ORANGES

2 CUPS CRANBERRIES, RAW

3 SOUR APPLES

1 CUP PINEAPPLE, GRATED

2 CUPS SUGAR

Remove peel from one orange. Put cranberries, oranges and apples through coarse cut of food grinder. Add pineapple and sugar and let stand in cool place 6 hours before using. Do not cook.

INDIA RELISH

8 POUNDS VERY SMALL GREEN TOMATOES

8 CUPS SUGAR (BROWN OR MAPLE)

2 CUPS WATER

3 STICKS CINNAMON

2 TABLESPOONS GINGER

3 LEMONS

2 CUPS CITRON, SHREDDED

3 CUPS SEEDED RAISINS

PEEL OF 1 SMALL ORANGE

Wash tomatoes and cut in quarters. Make syrup of sugar and water. Add tomatoes, cinnamon, ginger, lemons cut very thin, citron, raisins and orange peel. Boil slowly until fruit is clear. Pour into containers and seal. This is excellent with cold meat. South Union

The South Union Shaker community was especially famous for its canned goods and preserves. They often shipped large quantities of these as far distant as New Orleans and other southern markets. We read in their annals: "In a single day in the fall of 1856 the Sisters put up 300 jars of peaches. In 1872 in ten days besides washing, attending meetings and spinning 11,000 cocoons into silk thread, one single family of Sisters put up 3,917 jars of strawberry preserves . . . Then followed gooseberries, cherries, raspberries, blackberries, peaches, apples, quinces and grapes." This task of preserving was simply colossal when we consider most of it was done by hand, that the recipes were followed to the minutest detail and all the cooking was done on wood-burning stoves. Each jar passed the closest Shaker inspection and had to bear the stamp of perfection. The records state that at a most crucial time in mid-summer when their stove was weighted down with huge kettles of fragrant preserves, the great cast-iron stove cracked right down the center! What a calamity! Any

191

other cooks would have been relieved, but not the thrifty Shaker Sisters! Two Shaker brethren immediately drove to Cincinnati and bought a new stove, and the good work went right on! Not a berry or seed was wasted by these thrifty Early Americans.

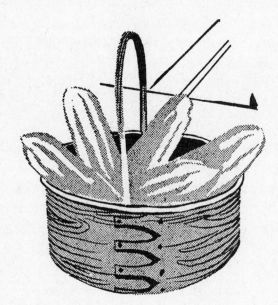

Preserves,
Jams, Jellies

In the history of food we might say jams and jellies are of rather recent origin, for these delicacies were not made until the refinement of white sugar became well established. In *Man's Food*, by Mark Graubard, we read that "sugar was mighty scarce two centuries ago; in 1750 white sugar cost $2.75 per pound." Consequently only the very wealthy could use it. At that time sugar came in a loaf or often in a cone-shape wrapped in blue paper. It was so expensive that it was kept in a small box, under lock and key, to which only the lady of the house had access. So precious was this commodity that when served with tea, small fragments were chipped off the loaf and held in the mouth while sipping the hot, fragrant brew.

In early antiquity India produced cane sugar in small amounts. Thence it found its way into Europe where Venice monopolized the sugar trade for centuries. After the discovery of the Americas, sugar cane was transplanted there, where it throve under sunny skies and slave labor. It was during Napoleon's regime that the sugar industry became established in Europe. Today beet and cane sugar are used interchangeably. Statistics show that twice as much beet sugar is manufactured.

In the early days of the American colonization, maple sugar was chiefly used in the northern section including Pennsylvania and Kentucky. It is said that the Quakers were largely responsible for this, for they refused to use the cane sugar which was produced under slave labor. Moreover, vast groves of maples grew in these states, which made maple sugar and syrup the cheapest possible sweetening available. The American Indian had developed this industry and soon taught it to the first settlers. Sorghum, a rich syrup made from the sorghum plant, and molasses produced from sugar cane were commonly used in baking and in making puddings and beverages but by no means lent themselves to making jams and jellies.

The Shakers, who were pioneers in the canning industry, probably started with their famous applesauce. This preserve did not require sugar, for it was made from dried apples and highly concentrated cider—boiled down to "a rich, thick dark syrup." This delicious Shaker concoction still lingers in the gustatory memory of a few old-timers as a "never-to-be-forgotten apple sass." They recall that the apple slices remained whole and floated in a rich dark juice of luscious flavor! Thousands upon thousands of gallons of this energy-producing confection were sealed in Shaker-made firkins and wooden pails and sent far and wide to American markets.

When white sugar became available, we read of one single Shaker community—South Union in Kentucky—preserving 960 jars of peach jam in a single day!

ॐ   ॐ

SHAKER APPLESAUCE

2 POUNDS DRIED APPLES

1/3 GALLON WATER

2/3 GALLON CIDER, BOILED DOWN FROM 2 GALLONS
   FRESH CIDER

1/2 POUND SUGAR (OPTIONAL)

Soak apples overnight in water. In the morning add the boiled-down cider to the soaked apples. Cover tightly and simmer for 3 1/2 hours; add sugar, if desired. Do not stir, for the apple slices should remain whole and float in the rich, dark syrup.   Sister Ethel Peacock, Sabbathday Lake

Or

2 POUNDS APPLES, BEN DAVIS OR MACINTOSH,
   PEELED AND SLICED THICK

2 GALLONS FRESH CIDER, BOILED DOWN TO 2/3 GALLON

1 CUP SUGAR (OPTIONAL)

Add apple slices to boiled-down cider; simmer until apples are tender. Do not stir, for apple slices must remain whole. Add sugar, if desired, but the concentrated cider is very sweet.

ॐ   ॐ

APPLE PARINGS JELLY

4 QUARTS APPLE PARINGS AND CORES

4 CUPS WATER

SUGAR

Wash apples thoroughly and glean parings and cores when

making apple pies, dumplings or dried apples. Be sure to use the cores, for they especially contain flavor and sweetness. Add water and simmer until fruit is soft. Strain through a jelly bag, but do not squeeze bag if you want jelly that is sparkling clear. Measure juice and add a cup of sugar for each cup of juice. Stir well and boil rapidly until mixture jells on spoon. Pour into jars and seal.　　　　　Amelia's Shaker Recipes

ဆာ　　　　　　　　　　　　　　　　　ﾌﾞ

The Shakers were famous orchardists; they cultivated several new species of apples, among which were the quince apple and a sweet variety which was especially adapted to drying and was used in their applesauce. Their fruit was the best obtainable; they cultivated their orchards and fertilized their trees thoroughly, and they trimmed their trees of all excess wood buds, which caused them to bear very heavily.

"As soon as the apple harvest opened in late August we often held several apple-paring bees a week when we often pared, quartered and sliced ten to twenty bushels for dried apples in a single evening. The Brethren joined us in this chore."—Sister Marcia, Mt. Lebanon

ဆာ　　　　　　　　　　　　　　　　　ﾌﾞ

SISTER LETTIE'S PEACH JELLY

6 POUNDS TREE-RIPENED PEACHES
1 CUP WATER
JUICE OF 2 LEMONS
SUGAR EQUAL TO AMOUNT OF JUICE

Wipe all the fuzz off the peaches, for it will cloud your jelly. Split the peaches (skins and all) in halves and remove pits. Crack a quarter of pits and crush kernels. Pack the peach halves in layers in large earthen jar and sprinkle with crushed kernels. Add water, cover tightly and place in a water bath

196

over a slow fire for several hours. Drip the juice through a jelly bag but do not squeeze, for that, too, will cloud the jelly. Add lemon juice to peach juice, and measure: add cup for cup of white sugar. Boil until it slides from spoon. Pour into containers and cover tightly.   Union Village

This is a painstaking process but the result is delicious. The crushed kernel adds tremendously to the flavor. This same recipe can be used for sour cherries, wild cherries or plums— with equal success. If wild cherries are used, grind one-third of the stemmed cherries with their pits; this gives the jell a delicious, pungent flavor. Excellent served with venison or wild fowl.

The first peaches appeared on market in this country in Boston in 1828. The peach originally came from China but was long raised in Europe before brought to America. A peach stone planted in good soil bore fruit in five years, while it took an apple tree from seven to eight years to mature. Tremendous peach orchards were planted in Ohio and Kentucky. . . . The sour cherry matured in three years; many cherry and peach pits were carried in the well-stuffed saddle-bags of the early pioneer, which paid off amply within a few years.

STRAWBERRY JAM

Use 1/2 pound of sugar to each pound of fruit. Put sugar in preserving kettle and add just enough water to make a heavy syrup. Cook until it strings off the spoon. Remove from fire and add fruit. Let stand 10 minutes. Strain off the berries in colander and set aside. Cook syrup again until it strings from spoon. Again add fruit and let stand in syrup for 10 minutes.

Repeat process; strain off berries and boil down syrup. Add fruit and boil gently for 15 minutes. Remove from fire and let stand 24 hours. Pour into scalded glasses, and wax. The fruit will never rise to the top if these rules are carefully followed; the berries will remain tender and retain their fresh fruit flavor. This method is especially satisfactory with strawberries and currants. Amelia's Shaker Recipes

To preserve lavender blossoms, put 2 pounds of the plucked blooms into a gallon of water and set them in a still over a very low fire. Distill gently until all water is exhausted. Repeat this process a second time. Then turn into scalded bottles and cork well.

SOUR CHERRY JAM

1/2 CUP CRACKED PITS
4 QUARTS SOUR CHERRIES, PITTED
3 QUARTS WHITE SUGAR

Add cracked pits tied in cheesecloth to the pitted cherries and sugar. Cook together for 1 1/2 hours, or until the jam thickens and the cherries take on a dark color. Remove bag of pits and pour jam into scalded jars and seal. This is a very rich and tasty confection. Amelia's Shaker Recipes

Fall challenged the wits of the Shaker Sisters to preserve the excess that was available, for use in the lean winter months. There were no factories producing canned foods nor were there suitable containers such as we have today. Jams had to be put up in any kind of available containers—often five-gallon crocks were used, or even wooden pails. The Shakers were pioneers in the canning industry. They also made most of their own containers, such as firkins, pails and kegs and barrels. In the early days the Sabbathday Lake Shakers made countless barrels for the flourishing molasses trade; later they made shaped barrel staves which they exported to the West Indies to molasses manufacturers.

It was not until the Civil War that canned goods became popular, but tin cans did not come into wide use until 1885, when a machine for stamping them out in great numbers was invented. Up to that date they had been made by hand and were very expensive.

CRANBERRY SAUCE

2 QUARTS CRANBERRIES
1 QUART BOILING WATER
1 QUART SUGAR

Discard poor fruit; pick over carefully and wash. Put berries in a preserving kettle with boiling water. Add sugar. Set on heat and simmer for 20 minutes. Stir often to prevent burning. This will not need straining and the rich full color will be preserved when cooked this way. Never cook cranberries without sugar—they lose their color and look very unappetizing.   Mary Whitcher's *Shaker Housekeeper*

Cranberries grew in great profusion along Doan Brook (now Lower Shaker Lakes, Cleveland). Many are the recipes found in the Shaker Household Journals for cranberry dumplings, puddings, sauces, tarts, cobblers, pies, relishes and even catsup. The Sisters also dried great quantities of them. Fruits were dried in the early days chiefly because of the lack of containers and also for lack of storage space. Dried fruit could be kept in bags and hung from the rafters of the cabins.

CRANBERRY CONSERVES

4 CUPS CRANBERRIES
2 ORANGES
2 CUPS HOT WATER
1 CUP RAISINS, SEEDED
4 CUPS SUGAR
1 CUP PECANS, CHOPPED

Grind the raw cranberries and oranges together. Add hot water and boil until fruit is tender; add raisins and sugar and simmer slowly until conserve thickens. Remove from heat and add nut meats. Pour into jars and seal.

ੈ෴   ෴ई

CONSERVE OF GRAPE

8 POUNDS CONCORD GRAPES, STEMMED
8 POUNDS SUGAR
1 1/2 POUNDS RAISINS, SEEDED
4 ORANGES
1 1/2 CUPS PECANS, CHOPPED

Remove skins and cook pulp of grapes until soft enough to run through colander to remove seeds. Combine pulp, skins, sugar, raisins, juice and grated rind of oranges and cook slowly until thick. Remove from heat and add nut meats. The original recipe called for black walnut or hickory meats, which were a drug on the market in the early days in Ohio when this recipe was compiled. Pecans would be the nearest substitute.   Sister Lisset, North Union

ੈ෴   ෴ई

TOMATO FIGS

8 POUNDS SMALL FIRM RIPE TOMATOES
2 POUNDS BROWN SUGAR

Scald tomatoes and remove skins. Cover with sugar and let stand 2 hours. Then simmer in their own juice until tomatoes are clarified. Do not stir or break tomatoes. Remove tomatoes from kettle and place on flat platter and gradually flatten by placing heavy platter on top. Weight down slightly. Remove platter and cover with syrup in which tomatoes were cooked. Cover with cheesecloth and let set several days. Sprinkle every morning with fine sugar and set in sun. At end of week sprinkle with sugar and pack in flat boxes. These are very delicious and taste almost like the best quality of figs. They keep well for a year. South Union

"The Brethren brought in a two-horse load of apples; tonight we all pared and cut for drying ten barrels of apples."—South Union

"At the Mill or North Family they raised a certain green plum which somewhat resembled a peach; the leaves of the trees exactly resembled the peach. This plum was especially fine for preserves. Every pit was saved and planted for these trees were in great demand in the vicinity."—From Daniel Boler's Journal, North Union

GREEN TOMATO PRESERVES

12 MEDIUM-SIZED GREEN TOMATOES

3 TABLESPOONS SALT

2 LEMONS, SLICED FINE

2 CUPS BROWN SUGAR

1 TEASPOON CLOVES, POWDERED

1 TEASPOON NUTMEG

1 TEASPOON ALLSPICE

Cube tomatoes and sprinkle well with salt; let stand overnight. Rinse and drain thoroughly and add lemons sliced as thin as paper. Add brown sugar and spices. Simmer for 2 hours. If you happen to have oil of spices in these particular flavors, use small quantities of the oil instead of the powdered spice, for this will give you a crystal-clear preserve. Seal in jars. Sister Annie Bell, Canterbury

SHAKER TOMATO JAM

4 POUNDS RIPE TOMATOES, SKINNED AND CHOPPED
16 CUPS SUGAR
4 LARGE ORANGES
8 LEMONS
3 STICKS CINNAMON

Scald tomatoes to remove skins, and chop fine. Add sugar, the juice and grated rind of oranges and lemons and cinnamon and cook until it jells on spoon. Skim, pour and seal. This makes a most appetizing, shocking-pink confection.

CARROT MARMALADE

3 CUPS CARROTS, BOILED AND CHOPPED
2 LEMONS
1 LARGE ORANGE
6 CUPS SUGAR

Boil carrots until just tender; drain well and chop fine, but do not put through food grinder. Add the juice and grated rind of lemons and orange, and sugar. Cook slowly for 1/2 hour or until it jells on spoon. Skim, pour and seal. Very delicious. Sister Mildred, Sabbathday Lake

Maple syrup like wine had its vintage years.

The American Colonists had molasses as soon as they began trading with the West Indies. The Maine Shakers made hundreds of barrels for this molasses trade.

Honey was used in ancient times to pay tithes, taxes and tributes. Strict property rights guarded all bees, and thefts of honey were punishable by death—which made it a crime on par with murder. Often all honey in the land belonged to the king in ancient times.

Salads

In DeGouy's *Salad Book* (1950) he says: "A salad is to a menu as a garden is to a home. Both delight the eye and refresh the spirit." The Shaker Sisters were not unmindful of the psychological effect of serving attractive-looking food—repeatedly they mention the necessity of making dishes "not only toothsome and nutritious but they must be dished-up in proper fashion to stimulate the appetite." It was the Shaker's satisfaction from tasks exceedingly well done that gave special excellence to their cookery and high standards to their dining service. Like their architecture, furniture and handicrafts, their cookery expressed quality and efficiency—in this humble art also, they were craftsmen with great pride in their craft. All the works of their hands reflected their zeal for millennial harmony or perfection. Their pride in their work was equal to that of the mediaeval craftsman!

In their Farm and Household Journals the Shakers often expressed endless delight with the simple gifts of fields and garden—the first tender sprouts of the dandelion, later the dock and mallow, the cress thriving along the brook. They gathered the despised weeds above mentioned and garnished and transformed them into palatable salads. They also used the tender tops of beets, turnips and radishes and converted them into tasty greens. Today we know how valuable greens are to man's health. Their Farm Journals state that from early spring and as "late as the middle of August a rotation of crops of beans, peas, spinach, beets and turnips can be planted in order to have crisp, fresh vegetables almost until the snow flies."

With the excellent refrigeration and rapid transportation of today, we get fresh vegetables at all times, and have no conception of how our forefathers must have craved leafy green vegetables throughout the long winter season. Primitive man ate herbs, barks and edible weeds to satisfy this craving which resulted from a heavy meat diet.

The Shaker annals do not list salads as a special course, but we find all sorts of suggestions on how to use cress, onions —ranging from shallots to leeks, the several lettuces they raised and celery which was used from root to top leaf. They raised large amounts of dandelions in their well-cultivated gardens, for not only were the young tender leaves used in salads and greens but the root also was highly valued for its medicinal properties.

In the Science News Letter of April 21, 1951, we read: "World hunger, which breeds revolution and unrest, could be conquered, if unusual foods—some of which are considered weeds—were more appreciated and utilized." Professor R. H. Harris of the Massachusetts Institute of Technology said at a meeting recently: "Experience has taught that certain weeds can provide the essentials of a good diet, as well as meat, milk and eggs which we consider so necessary. Iron, calcium and needed vitamins can be obtained from what we consider weeds."

Here is an ancient salad claimed to be, "A Favorite Sallet (salad) of Kings," often called "King Richard II's Sallet." This tasty dish proves that our ancestors appreciated greens and herbs and that they could take a lusty combination of them. It is little wonder they could wield the lance and battleaxe after consuming this dish! The recipe reads: "Take parsel (parsley), sawge (sage), garlic, chiballas (spring onions), leeks, borage, myntes (mints), fenel, and ten tressis (water cress), rew (rue) and rosemayre. Wash hyme clene and pluck hyme small with thyne handes and lave hyme with raw oil. Lay red wyne thereon and salt and parkake well." (Circa 1370)

EARLY SPRING SALAD

4 CUPS DANDELION LEAVES, CUT

4 SLICES BACON

1/2 CUP VINEGAR

2 TABLESPOONS SUGAR

1/4 CUP WATER

1 TEASPOON SALT

1/4 TEASPOON PEPPER

1 TABLESPOON ONION, CHOPPED

4 HARD-COOKED EGGS

Carefully pick over the first dandelion leaves and cut in 2 inch lengths. They must be gathered before the plant blooms. In a skillet fry the bacon crisp; remove from pan; keep fat to which add vinegar, sugar, water, salt and pepper and stir until well blended. Cool and toss dressing through greens and onion. Heap salad in mound and garnish with strips of bacon and slices of egg. This is a good appetizer. Serves 6.

North Union

"One of the first signs of spring is the tiny sawlike leaf of the dandelion sticking its leaves above the thawing earth. Before they have a chance to burst into bloom, have the children gather these succulent plants. This furnishes you with a tasty dish and at the same time rids your door yard of a weed."

"To make a good salad four persons are wanted; a spendthrift to furnish the oil, a miser to measure the vinegar, a councillor to dole out the salt and spice, and a madman to toss it!"   —*Shaker Manifesto*

CUCUMBER SALAD

2 CUCUMBERS
1/2 ONION
1/2 CUP SOUR CREAM
1/2 CUP VINEGAR
1/2 TEASPOON SALT
1/4 TEASPOON PEPPER
2 TABLESPOONS SUGAR
1/4 TEASPOON MUSTARD

Select tender young cucumbers; peel one but leave the other unpeeled. Slice very fine. Sprinkle with salt and let stand just three minutes, thus removing any bitter taste of the skin. Mix dressing of sour cream, vinegar and seasoning and pour over cucumbers. Serve at once for full flavor. Serves 6.

Amelia's Shaker Recipes

"It does not seem to be generally known that the cucumber is one of the most valuable vegetables we raise. It can be dressed in more palatable and suitable ways than most any other vegetable except tomatoes. It is far better than squash and more delicate than eggplant when stewed, fried or stuffed and is most delicious when made into fritters in a dainty batter. Even when they have become too old to be served as salad and too tough for pickling, it is then the cucumber is at its best for cooking. . . . Let your cucumbers lay in cold water for an hour before peeling. Always begin peeling at the small end and peel toward the stem end. . . . Cucumbers can be kept into late winter by packing them with sand in wooden boxes with drainage holes in the bottom. By no means let them touch one another. Cover tightly and keep in a very cold, well-ventilated cellar. These will add a great variety to the winter diet of root vegetables. . . . Cucumbers want herbs! They are excellent appetizers. Do not wilt them before dressing, for it makes them look unappetizing. Try serving them freshly cut from the garden, peeled and cut and dressed with minced dill and salt and pepper. . . ."—Shaker *Manifesto*

SISTER LETTIE'S BEET SALAD

2 TABLESPOONS SUGAR

1 TEASPOON SALT

1 TEASPOON MUSTARD

1/2 CUP VINEGAR

6 COOKED BEETS, SLICED

4 HARD-COOKED EGGS

4 SMALL ONIONS

2 GREEN PEPPERS

Make a dressing by combining sugar, salt, mustard and vinegar. Heat and pour over sliced beets. When cool add the whole hard-cooked eggs (shells removed) and let stand overnight. Arrange sliced beets in center of dish and surround with rings of sliced onions and garnish with slices of pickled egg. Dress with lettuce and slices of green peppers. Pour some of the dressing over the salad and serve. Serves 6.

"Endive, lettuce, parsley, leeks, shallots, cress, dandelion and small spinach leaves are all green salad materials and should be gathered fresh from the garden and used when crisp and flavorful. . . ."—Shaker Recipe

Today much is said on this subject of freshness, for scientists have learned that greens and leafy vegetables lose much of their food values by wilting.

GARDEN SALADS

Rub your wooden salad bowl with a clove of garlic. Toss into it very young leaves of spinach, the inside tender stalks of celery, the flowers plucked from a head of cauliflower and baby carrots only two inches long. Wash well, dry and pour over them olive oil and red wine vinegar; sprinkle with salt and pepper.

Skin six medium-sized tomatoes and chill. Slice them on a bed of crisp lettuce leaves and serve with favorite dressing. This is the best of all salads!

Slice red and white radishes on the slaw cutter and serve on lettuce leaves with boiled dressing (see end of chapter).

"Beets, cabbage, chard, chicory, endive, turnip leaves and all the wild greens such as dandelions, lamb's quarters, dock and mustard all are very succulent grub when properly combined and dressed. There are many delicious treats awaiting you in the fields if you learn to recognize and use them. Sour sorrel is another tasty plant one should not overlook for flavor in salads. . . . Borage—its first tender leaves when added to salads awaken in one a new sense of joy that spring is again here! Its wooly leaves and twinkling blue flowers add much interest to the herb garden but far more to the salad bowl. And there is lamb's lettuce, a blunt-leafed, clumpy little salad plant which lasts late into the fall and can be covered with straw and used throughout the winter. . . ."—Gleanings from Shaker Accounts

CORN SALAD

12 EARS COOKED CORN
1/2 HEAD CABBAGE
4 SWEET RED PEPPERS
1 BUNCH CELERY
1 1/2 TABLESPOONS SALT
1 CUP VINEGAR
1 CUP WATER
1 1/2 TABLESPOONS DRY MUSTARD

When cold, cut corn off the cob. Chop celery, cabbage and peppers fine; cook together for 10 minutes and drain. Mix vegetables; add salt, vinegar and water and moistened mustard. (Some cooks add 1/2 cup sugar.) Bring to a boil and cook 20 minutes. Seal in containers. It goes well with any dinner.   Union Village

CABBAGE SALAD

1 QUART CABBAGE, SLICED OR CHOPPED
1/2 CUP THICK SWEET CREAM

2 TABLESPOONS SUGAR

1 TEASPOON SALT

1/4 TEASPOON PEPPER

2 TABLESPOONS STRONG VINEGAR OR LEMON JUICE

A nice way to prepare raw cabbage salad is as follows: Select a firm, solid head; chop fine or cut on slaw cutter as much as you judge you need. To every quart of cabbage add 1/2 cup of thick sweet cream, 2 tablespoons sugar, 1/2 teaspoon salt and 2 tablespoons vinegar or lemon juice. Toss thoroughly and serve.

SHAKER POTATO SALAD

6 MEDIUM POTATOES, COOKED IN SKINS

3 SLICES BACON

1 MEDIUM-SIZED ONION, MINCED

1/2 TEASPOON SALT

DASH OF PEPPER

1 TABLESPOON SUGAR

1/2 CUP VINEGAR

1 TABLESPOON PARSLEY, MINCED

3 HARD-COOKED EGGS

2 BUNCHES LEAF LETTUCE, CRISPED

Boil potatoes in the skins. When just cool enough to peel, remove skins and slice fine. Try out finely cut bacon. Add onion, minced fine; simmer until golden but not brown. Add salt, pepper, sugar and vinegar to hot bacon fat. Heat and turn this hot dressing over warm potatoes. Turn salad on a bed of lettuce leaves and sprinkle generously with minced parsley; dress up the salad with quarters of hard-cooked eggs. This served with cold meat and cheese is a mighty satisfactory supper. Serves 6.   Amelia's Shaker Recipes

Salad hints from Shaker Manifesto:

"Salads should always be served as soon as possible after preparing them. Salads should be tossed or blended very lightly with a couple of wooden forks; never pack or mash them."

"To fringe celery, cut in four-inch lengths; stick several sewing needles into a cork and comb celery with it. Throw in very cold water to curl. This makes a pretty dish."

"Rings made from the whites of hard-cooked eggs are a nice garnish for salad."

"Pick over and carefully wash your cress to remove all slugs and sand. Arrange in a deep dish and serve with spiced vinegar."

SHAKER CARROT SALAD

2 EGGS

1 TEASPOON SALT

1/8 TEASPOON CAYENNE PEPPER

2 TEASPOONS DRY MUSTARD

2 TABLESPOONS BUTTER

1 CUP VINEGAR

2 CUPS CARROTS, BOILED AND DICED

2 CUPS CHESTNUTS, PARBOILED

1/2 CUP SWEET PEPPERS, CHOPPED

2 CLUMPS (BUNCHES) GARDEN LETTUCE

Make a boiled dressing by beating eggs and adding seasoning, butter and vinegar and stirring over a very low fire until thickened and smooth. When cold mix with carrots, diced chestnuts and peppers. Turn out on crisp lettuce leaves and serve. Serves 6.   Sister Melissa, Watervliet, Ohio

SALMON SALAD

2 CUPS CANNED OR COOKED SALMON
1/2 CUP CELERY, DICED
1/2 CUP CABBAGE, SHREDDED
1/4 CUP GREEN PEPPERS, SHREDDED
1/2 TEASPOON SALT
1/8 TEASPOON PAPRIKA
LETTUCE
3 HARD-COOKED EGGS

Break salmon in inch cubes. Add vegetables and extra seasoning. Moisten with boiled dressing (see below) and serve on lettuce. Garnish with sliced eggs.

FRESH FRUIT SALAD

3 CUPS RIPE PEARS, DICED
3 CUPS PEACHES, DICED
1 CUP TART APPLE, DICED
1 CUP WHITE GRAPES
1 CUP MAYONNAISE
1 CUP HEAVY CREAM
BED OF SHREDDED LETTUCE

Pare pears, peaches and apple and cut in half-inch dices. Do not mince food for salads, for it looks very unappetizing after dressing is added. Add grapes. Blend mayonnaise with cream and add to fruit. Serve cold on bed of lettuce.

Amelia's Shaker Recipes

HERB SALAD DRESSING

1 TABLESPOON ONION, MINCED
1/2 TEASPOON SALT
1/2 TEASPOON DRY MUSTARD
1/8 TEASPOON PEPPER
1 TABLESPOON THYME, MINCED
1 TABLESPOON SUMMER SAVORY, MINCED
3 TABLESPOONS TARRAGON VINEGAR
6 TABLESPOONS OLIVE OIL

Add onion, salt, mustard, pepper, thyme and savory to vinegar and blend in the oil.

BOILED DRESSING

1/4 TEASPOON DRY MUSTARD
1 TEASPOON SALT
1 TEASPOON SUGAR
1/8 TEASPOON PEPPER
DASH OF CAYENNE
3 EGG YOLKS
1 CUP OF EQUAL PARTS OF VINEGAR AND WATER
1 TABLESPOON BUTTER

Mix the dry ingredients and stir into well-beaten egg yolks. Add the water and vinegar and stir well. Put in top of double boiler and cook until thickened. Add butter and let cool before using. A cup of heavy or sour cream can be whipped into this dressing. This dressing is especially good on potato, cabbage or other vegetable salads.   Amelia's Shaker Recipes

OIL SALAD DRESSING

1 TEASPOON SALT

2 TEASPOONS SUGAR

1/2 TEASPOON PAPRIKA

1/2 TEASPOON DRY MUSTARD

4 TABLESPOONS VINEGAR OR LEMON JUICE

3 EGG YOLKS

2 CUPS OLIVE OR SALAD OIL

Mix dry ingredients and moisten with vinegar or lemon juice. Beat egg yolks and blend with seasoning mixture. Add oil drop by drop at first and beat until thickened.

Soups

Long before Esau bartered away his birthright for a bowl of
pottage (lentil soup), man had learned the art of soup-
making—stretching his meager food supply by boiling them
in liquids. We are told in MacLean's *Shakers of Ohio* that
when the Whitewater community was formed in Ohio, "The
Shakers had neither hogs nor money with which to purchase
meat. Their common manner was to buy a side of bacon
when able, and make sop for their johnny cake. This was
made by mixing water and milk with the finely cut meat and
boiling it with meal. This they used morning and noon. . . ."

In the early days at North Union and probably at the

other western Shaker communities the great iron soup pot was kept handy by the constantly glowing fire, and into it went the trimmings of meat, bones of roasts and the broth from all their cooked vegetables. At the end of the day this broth was strained and used in the making of stews and gravy on the morrow. However, lamb and mutton seldom went into this pot for they are too strong in flavor, while pork is too rich and sweet to make good stock.

Like all good cooks, the Shaker kitchen Sisters classified soups in three groups: *thin, clear soups* which stimulate appetite and are known as consommé, bouillion and broth; *thin cream soups* called bisques and vegetable broths; and *heavy thick soups* and *chowders*.

In the making of the thin, clear soups, uncooked meat and split or cracked bones are the basis. The meat and bones are covered with cold water to which salt has been added to extract nourishment and cooked very slowly for several hours in a covered kettle. Vegetables are added the last half hour. These soups are clarified before serving and are used as an appetizer to a dinner.

The second group, the thin cream soups, are the ideal preface to a dinner or as a main supper or lunch dish, especially for children or the aged. There is an almost endless variety of this kind. They can be made from cooked strained vegetables to which a thin cream sauce has been added, or they may be slightly thickened by adding the yolk of egg or cooked cereal such as rice, barley or tapioca.

The third group, the heavy thick soups and chowders, should never be served with a dinner, for they are a meal in themselves. They are made of fish, meat and vegetables with cream sauce or milk and cracker thickening. Purée of peas, beans, tomatoes and lentils are excellent thickeners for soup of this type.

Soup need never become a commonplace dish, for the

garnishes and the accompanying crackers, croutons, bread-sticks, toasts and cheese straws challenge any cook's imagination and ingenuity. It is amazing to read what all the Shaker Sisters converted into soups, broths and chowders!

ૐ   ✑

WHITE OR VEAL STOCK

4 POUNDS VEAL KNUCKLE, BONE CRACKED
NECKS AND FEET OF 2 CHICKENS
4 QUARTS COLD WATER
2 MEDIUM-SIZED ONIONS, QUARTERED
2 CARROTS, SCRUBBED AND QUARTERED
1 STALK CELERY
12 SPRIGS PARSLEY
1 SPRIG THYME
2 BAY LEAVES
12 PEPPERCORNS, BRUISED
1 TABLESPOON SALT
1 BLADE OF MACE

Skin chicken feet by scalding. Place veal and chicken parts in soup pot with cold water and let stand an hour to draw out nutriment. Place kettle over low flame and let come to a gentle boil. Simmer very gently for 3 1/2 hours, skimming frequently. Add onions, carrots, celery, parsley and seasoning and simmer for another half hour. Strain and when cold remove film of fat on top. Let ripen for 12 hours before serving. If not sufficiently clear, heat and add shell and white of 1 egg and simmer for 5 minutes.   Amelia's Shaker Recipes

ૐ   ✑

SHAKER BEEF BROTH

2 OX-TAILS
1 KNUCKLE OF VEAL

1 GALLON COLD WATER

1 TABLESPOON SALT

12 PEPPERCORNS, BRUISED

2 CARROTS, QUARTERED

4 CELERY ROOTS

4 STALKS CELERY, LEAVES AND ALL (UNCURLED KIND)

HANDFUL OF SOUP PARSLEY

4 GREEN ONIONS, TOPS AND ALL

1 BLADE MACE

2 BAY LEAVES

1 SPRIG THYME

Place the oxtails and the knuckle of veal in the soup pot; add the cold water and let stand for 1 hour. The veal knuckle adds body or gelatin to the soup and also imparts a rich flavor which beef alone will not give. Set pot over medium heat and let come to a boil; skim well. Reduce heat and let simmer for 3 1/2 hours, after which add vegetables, herbs and seasoning. Simmer another half hour and strain through cheesecloth-lined sieve. When cold remove all fat from top. Let ripen 24 hours before using.   Eldress Clymena Miner, North Union

SISTER LUELLA'S CHICKEN BROTH

3 PAIRS CHICKEN FEET, SKINNED

1 STEWING HEN, CUT UP

3 QUARTS COLD WATER

1 CARROT, CUT IN INCH PIECES

2 STALKS CELERY, LEAVES AND ALL

2 GREEN ONIONS, TOPS AND ALL

6 SPRIGS SOUP PARSLEY

1 TEASPOON SALT

6 PEPPERCORNS, BRUISED

Scald the chicken feet and remove skin and claws. Toss into

the soup pot along with the chicken. The feet add the needed gelatin and give body to the broth. Add water and let come to a boil over slow fire. Skim well and cover pot and let simmer for 2 1/2 hours, skimming occasionally. Then add carrot, celery, onions, parsley and seasoning and simmer another 20 minutes. Strain through sieve covered with cheesecloth. When cold, remove any fat formed on top. This makes an excellent basis for many kinds of soup. The meat can be removed from bones and used in salads or jellied chicken with additional seasoning and salad dressing added.

SPRING VEGETABLE SOUP

1 TABLESPOON BUTTER

2 LEEKS

3 STALKS CELERY

3 SPRIGS SOUP PARSLEY

2 PARSLEY ROOTS

1/4 CUP GREEN PEPPER, CHOPPED

1 CUP LETTUCE, SHREDDED

2 QUARTS CHICKEN BROTH (SEE ABOVE)

16 SLICES RAW POTATO

1 CARROT, SLICED

Melt butter and add sliced leeks, celery and parsley, but do not brown. Blanch the green pepper and lettuce in boiling water for 1 minute. Heat broth and pour over vegetables including potato and carrot. Add seasoning and cook slowly for 20 minutes. Serve very hot with toasted crackers. Serves 4-6.

Amelia's Shaker Recipes

Today we cannot imagine what it meant to the early Shakers (or to our forefathers) to taste the first green sprouts after the long winter diet of root-vegetables, dried corn and salt-meats! Because the first green sprouts were so scarce and precious, they very often went into the soup pot, there to be stretched into plenty for the large household; in the soup pot all the delicacy of flavor was converted into satisfaction to the palate.

ੈੈ   ৼ

SHAKER HERB SOUP

1 TABLESPOON BUTTER
2 TABLESPOONS CHIVES, CHOPPED
2 TABLESPOONS CHERVIL, MINCED
2 TABLESPOONS SORREL, MINCED
1/2 TEASPOON TARRAGON, CUT FINE
1 CUP CELERY, CUT FINE
1 QUART CHICKEN BROTH (SEE ABOVE)
SALT AND PEPPER TO TASTE
SUGGESTION OF SUGAR
6 SLICES OF TOAST
DASH OF NUTMEG
GRATED CHEESE

Put butter in skillet; when melted add minced herbs and celery and simmer for 3 minutes. Add broth and seasoning. Cook gently for 20 minutes. Place slices of toast in tureen and pour soup over them; add nutmeg and sprinkle with grated cheese. Serve very hot. Serves 4-6.

Amelia's Shaker Recipes

Household Hints on Shaker Soups
All heavy fats should be trimmed from meats and fowl before they go into soup pot, for fats flatten the flavor of soups.

Skimming soup during cooking is very important if you wish a fine clear broth.

Broths may be made from fresh meat or fish, or from

roast bones or turkey carcasses, but the latter will not make a clear broth and should be used only as a base for cream soups.

Combinations of herbs in soups are endless and make an interesting study.

For broths, always start the soup with cold water; this will extract the greatest nourishment from the ingredients in your pot.

Try a dash of nutmeg and a pinch of sugar in most any soup!

As an introduction to a good book whets one's interest in what is to follow, just so should a clear soup stimulate and enliven the most jaded appetite for a good dinner!

ELDRESS CLYMENA'S TOMATO SOUP

24 MEDIUM-SIZED RIPE TOMATOES

2 STALKS CELERY, CUT

2 TABLESPOONS GREEN PEPPERS, MINCED

2 BAY LEAVES

1 TEASPOON SALT

1 TEASPOON SUGAR

DASH OF CAYENNE

1 TABLESPOON PARSLEY, MINCED

1/4 TEASPOON ONION JUICE

1/2 TEASPOON LEMON JUICE

1/2 CUP WHIPPED CREAM

DASH OF SALT

Do not skin tomatoes; cut in quarters and place in heavy pot with celery, green pepper and bay leaves. Cover tightly and simmer 20 minutes without adding any water. Pass through a sieve; add seasoning and let come to boiling point. Pour into hot bowls and top with whipped cream slightly salted. Excellent! Serves 6.

OYSTER STEW

2 PINTS OYSTERS

4 TABLESPOONS BUTTER

1 TEASPOON SALT

1/4 TEASPOON PEPPER (WHITE PREFERRED)

2 CUPS MILK

2 CUPS CREAM

1 TABLESPOON PARSLEY, MINCED

To the oysters and their liquid add the butter, salt and pepper. Stew over very low heat for 12 minutes, stirring frequently. Add milk and cream and simmer until oysters curl slightly at edges. Serve in a heated china tureen with as little delay as possible. Dust top with the minced parsley. Serve toasted soda crackers with the stew. Do not make in an iron pot, for it may discolor stew; a new granite stew pan should be used in making this delicate soup. Some cooks prefer removing the hard muscle of the oyster. Serves 6-8.

Mary Whitcher's *Shaker Housekeeper*

OKRA SOUP

1/4 POUND SALT PORK, CUT FINE

2 CUPS OKRA, SLICED FINE

1 CUP GREEN PEPPER, DICED

1 CUP CELERY, DICED

1 LARGE RIPE TOMATO

4 CUPS BOILING WATER

1 TEASPOON SALT

1 TEASPOON DARK BROWN SUGAR

1/4 TEASPOON PAPRIKA

Try out the cut salt pork in soup pot. Simmer vegetables in hot fat. Add water and seasoning and simmer until vegetables are tender (about 30 minutes). Cooked chicken cut in neat cubes enhances this dish considerably. Serves 4.

Amelia's Shaker Recipes

ह‍ॐ   ॐ‍ई

ELDRESS MARY WHITCHER'S OKRA SOUP

2 VEAL KNUCKLES
2 LARGE ONIONS, DICED
2 CARROTS, DICED
4 TOMATOES, SKINNED AND CUT
4 1/2 QUARTS WATER
1 TEASPOON SALT
1/2 TEASPOON SUGAR
1/8 TEASPOON PEPPER
1 QUART OKRA, CUT FINE

Split knuckles with cleaver and put in soup pot with onions, carrots and tomatoes; add water and seasoning. Simmer for 6 1/2 hours. Remove knuckles and cut good meat into cubes and return to pot. Take the glutinous part of meat and grind it into jelly and add to soup. Now add the sliced okra and simmer for 30 more minutes. This okra soup equals any turtle soup. Serve very hot. Serves 8.

ह‍ॐ   ॐ‍ई

"This soup is a meal in itself and should not be served with a dinner but as a supper (or luncheon) dish along with some greens and a hearty dessert."

Mary Whitcher's life was as rich and life-giving as her good soup recipes. She and her husband, Benjamin, lived on a hundred-acre ancestral farm near Canterbury, New Hampshire, when in 1782 they were converted by two Shaker missionaries from New Lebanon. For ten years they gathered Shaker converts under their hospitable roof, which was converted into the Canterbury Shaker communty in 1792. Benjamin became the Elder of this first family or unit, and Mary was chosen as one of the Trustees; in this capacity she served until her death in 1797. Her small booklet, entitled Mary Whitcher's *Shaker Housekeeper,* has become very rare and is occasionally listed, today, in book catalogues at $100.

ह♥   ♥ई

TURTLE SOUP
2 POUND VEAL KNUCKLE
1/2 CUP BUTTER
1 CARROT, DICED
2 SMALL ONIONS, DICED
1 STALK CELERY, CUT
2 CLOVES
1 BAY LEAF
1/2 CUP FLOUR
2 QUARTS LIGHT BEEF STOCK
1 CUP TOMATOES, COOKED AND STRAINED
MEAT OF A SNAPPING TURTLE, CUBED
1 CUP SHERRY COOKING WINE
2 SPRIGS THYME
2 SPRIGS MARJORAM
SALT AND PEPPER
2 SLICES LEMON
DASH OF TABASCO
1 HARD-COOKED EGG

Break the knuckle with a cleaver and place in roasting pan with butter, carrot, onions, celery, cloves, bay leaf. Roast to a nice light brown in a hot oven. Add flour and mix well; bake 20 minutes longer. Remove baked mixture to soup kettle; add stock and tomato and simmer for 3 hours. Combine turtle meat, sherry, thyme, marjoram, salt and pepper, lemon and tabasco and cook slowly 10 minutes. Strain the stock mixture and add to the turtle mixture. Add the chopped egg and more sherry, if desired. Serve at once. Serves 8.

ॐ   ঞ্চ

OLD-FASHIONED POTATO SOUP

4 POUNDS SMALL POTATOES

2 TABLESPOONS CARAWAY SEED

2 TEASPOONS SALT

2 QUARTS WATER

6 SMALL LEEKS, CHOPPED

2 QUARTS MILK

2 TABLESPOONS MARJORAM, CHOPPED FINE

1 TEASPOON PAPRIKA

6 STRIPS CRISP BACON, MINCED

Scrub the potatoes thoroughly. Do not peel but place in soup pot whole with caraway seed, salt and water. Cook for half an hour, very slowly. Peel potatoes and cut fine; put back into pot with liquor in which they were cooked (the peelings add greatly to the flavor and nourishment). Add the leeks, top and all, cut fine. Cook for half an hour and pass through coarse sieve. Add milk. Heat well. Add marjoram, paprika and more salt, if necessary. Garnish with minced crisp bacon. Serve with toasted crackers. Serves 8.

Mary Whitcher's *Shaker Housekeeper*

ॐ   ঞ্চ

GREEN CORN SOUP

2 CUPS CORN, FRESHLY GRATED

2 CUPS WATER

1 TEASPOON SALT

1/8 TEASPOON PEPPER

1/2 TEASPOON SUGAR

2 TABLESPOONS BUTTER

1 TABLESPOON FLOUR

2 CUPS RICH MILK

1 ONION, WHOLE

Grate and scrape the corn from the cob; boil in water 5 minutes. Add salt, pepper and sugar. Melt butter in skillet and blend in flour; mix with milk and combine the two mixtures. Drop in the whole onion and cook slowly for 10 minutes. Remove onion and serve very hot with crisp crackers. Serves 6.

Mary Whitcher's *Shaker Housekeeper*

SHAKER PEASE PORRIDGE

2 CUPS SPLIT PEAS

1 QUART STOCK

2 ONIONS OR LEEKS, DICED

2 CARROTS, DICED

2 STALKS CELERY, CUT

1 TURNIP, DICED

1 TEASPOON SALT

1/4 TEASPOON PEPPER

Soak peas overnight. Simmer in stock for 2 hours; add onions, carrots, celery, turnip and seasoning and cook slowly another 30 minutes. Pass through a coarse sieve. Serve very hot with well-buttered rye bread croutons. Serves 4.

"Some like it hot and some like it cold . . ." Since the Shaker Sabbath started at sundown on Saturday, and since they kept the Sabbath very holy unto the Lord, as little cooking as possible was done on Sunday. Consequently such dishes as pease porridge, baked beans and puddings which improved with long baking in the great brick ovens were favorite Sabbath food in the early days.

ᢞ   ᢤ

BEAN SOUP

2 CUPS NAVY BEANS

A HAM BONE (NOT TOO WELL TRIMMED)

3 QUARTS WATER

2 CUPS CELERY, DICED

1 CUP ONION, CHOPPED

4 RIPE TOMATOES, CUT IN QUARTERS

1 CUP POTATOES, DICED

SALT AND PEPPER

1 TABLESPOON PARSLEY, MINCED

Soak beans overnight and drain in morning. Add ham bone and water and cook slowly until beans are soft. Add vegetables and cook another 20 minutes. Put through coarse sieve. Taste for seasoning, for ham may be salty. Season to taste and add minced parsley. Serve very hot with fried bread fingers. Serves 6-8.   Old North Union

ᢞ   ᢤ

SHAKER FISH CHOWDER

1/2 POUND SALT PORK, CUT FINE

2 ONIONS, MINCED

4 POUNDS FRESH FISH, FILLETED AND CUT

2 CUPS RAW POTATOES, SLICED FINE

1/2 TEASPOON SALT

1/8 TEASPOON PEPPER

2 TABLESPOONS FLOUR

1 PINT SCALDED MILK

8 HARD CRACKERS (WATER BISCUITS)

Put the pork in a skillet and fry slowly for 12 minutes; add the onion and fry to a very light yellow. (Do not brown.) Cut fish fillets into inch squares. Place a layer of fish and a layer of potatoes over sautéd onions; dredge lightly with salt, pepper and flour. Repeat until fish is used up. Cover with boiling water and cook for 15 minutes. Add a pint of scalded rich milk and split crackers and cook 30 minutes. Serve very hot. Do not use a bland fish for chowder; red snapper, fresh salmon, mullet or clams are tastiest. Some like to add a bouquet of garden herbs, which is removed before serving.

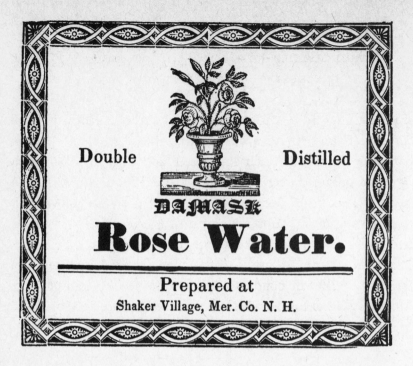

Double   Distilled

DAMASK

Rose Water.

Prepared at

Shaker Village, Mer. Co. N. H.

Sweetmeats

In the chapter on Jams and Jellies the story is told of the scarcity of sugar in the early days. Although the process of sugar-making was well understood in India as early as the first century, the refining involved the use of bone-ash which caused the product to be tabooed among the natives. Sugar was, however, used for medicinal purposes among the Hindu. By the eighth century the Arabs had carried the secret of the process into Egypt and Mesopotamia and then on into Spain. From thence sugar cane was shipped to the West Indies and other tropical regions of the Americas in the sixteenth century. Not until the beet sugar industry became established in the nineteenth century, did sugar become a reasonably priced commodity.

Honey, Nature's most delectable contribution to the food of man, was highly prized by the ancients. To the ancient Hebrew it was a symbol of abundance. It was equally prized by our early settlers in America, including the Shakers. In the annals of the Russell family, who were the founders of North Union, we read of their traveling on foot in the dead of winter to Solon, Ohio—a distance of thirty some miles—to buy a few bushels of wheat. While there they found a huge iron "hog-scalding pot" which they purchased and hauled back home on their sledge. Passing through a woods they discovered a "bee-tree"—the contents of which soon filled their newly acquired pot and made the trip a real occasion in their pioneer lives!

When the Shaker honey supply was low, they spread some on a heated stone; almost immediately the bees scented the fragrance and were soon seen buzzing about the bait. A boy, fleet of foot, was in hiding close by. He followed the bees to their lair and soon extracted the needed sweet from the bee-tree. Later, North Union erected a bee-house and cultivated bees. In fact, the only remaining building of their three good-sized villages on their vast farm is a frame bee-house which was built about 1875 for one of their founders, Brother Riley Honey. This founder is said to have been the first white child born on the Western Reserve. He grew up to wield an ax, erect a cabin, boil down sugar water, catch coons and find wild honey better than any in these parts! After a lifetime of loyal service to the Shaker community, this pioneer Brother became deaf and could no longer serve his community as trustee. The community set up the bee-house and for over a decade Riley Honey carried on a flourishing trade. The little discarded bee-house is a fitting memorial to the Shaker Brother who silently carried on his new trade until death claimed him at eighty-six.

Other important sugar products used by the Shakers were maple syrup and maple sugar. In the July, 1906, issue of *Good Housekeeping* in an article on "Shaker Industries," by Sister Marcia of Mt. Lebanon, we glean this first-hand description of sugar-making back in the 1860's: "Near our village was a grove of nearly 1,000 trees, so the making of sugar and syrup was an important industry. The camp was on the side of a hill and two miles from the village and here the great sheet-iron kettles were arranged over fires. . . . At the first sign of spring a detachment of Sisters went out and washed the wooden buckets before they could be hung on the trees. The sap was brought into camp and boiled down by the Brethren and then brought in on ox-sleds to the sugar-shop when the Sisters took over the rest of the task. Shaker syrup is remarkably fine because it is clarified by the addition of milk—a quart to every twelve gallons of syrup, but it must be put in at just the right moment to produce the right result.

"The syrup was stored in 2 gallon jugs, sealed with resin. . . . The Sisters also made quantities of little scalloped maple sugar cakes for sale. Then when all the sale sugar was finished, the Sisters made candy for the family; each member being allowed a pound—plain, flavored or mixed to suit their fancy. The flavors were wintergreen, mint, clove, cinnamon or hoarhound. . . .

"Finally, when the last of the sap was gathered, there came a day of bucket washing. We started very early in the morning, the younger Sisters walking and the older ones with the lunch coming on the ox-sleds. When we reached the camp we found roaring fires under the great sap-kettles to supply us with hot water, for it was no small chore to wash a thousand sticky wooden pails. However, we fell to and scrubbed and rinsed with an honest will, for when they were all clean and all stacked in their own particular shed, we had our playtime! The more sedate Sisters walked among the trees and communed with Nature but the younger ones swung on the branches and played bean bags and romped like real girls. Such days in the woods did not come to us often and we made the most of them. . . ."

SHAKER MOLASSES TAFFY

1 CUP MOLASSES

1 CUP SUGAR

1 CUP THIN CREAM

2 TABLESPOONS BUTTER

1 TEASPOON SODA

1 CUP CHOPPED BLACK WALNUTS

Cook molasses, sugar and cream until a ball is formed when dropped in cold water. Remove from heat and add butter and soda and chopped nuts. Pour on a buttered platter until cool enough to pull. When hard, cut into desired lengths.

North Union

TAFFY

1 CUP SUGAR

1/2 CUP HONEY

1/8 TEASPOON SALT

1 TABLESPOON BUTTER

Cook all ingredients together until a ball is formed when dropped in cold water. Pour on buttered platter until cool enough to pull. Butter hands and pull until hard.

North Union

HOARHOUND CANDY

3 CUPS BOILING WATER

3 OUNCES HOARHOUND LEAVES

6 CUPS DARK BROWN SUGAR

1 TEASPOON BUTTER

1 TEASPOON CREAM OF TARTAR

1 TEASPOON LEMON JUICE

Pour the boiling water over the chopped hoarhound leaves and let steep 20 minutes. Strain off tea and add sugar, cream of tartar and butter and cook until syrup forms hard ball when dropped in water. Add lemon juice and remove from fire. Pour on buttered plate and cut in small squares before too hard. North Union

MAPLE CREAMS

3 CUPS MAPLE SUGAR

1 CUP CREAM

1/2 TEASPOON MAPLE FLAVORING

1 CUP CHOPPED BUTTERNUTS

Cook sugar and cream until a soft ball is formed when tested in cold water. Cool and beat until very creamy. Add maple flavoring. Have platter buttered and sprinkled with nut meats and pour maple cream over nuts. When cold, cut in squares.

CANDIED MINT LEAVES

WHITE OF AN EGG

3 DROPS OIL OF PEPPERMINT
1/2 CUP POWDERED SUGAR
2 CUPS FRESH MINT LEAVES

Slightly beat egg white. Mix oil of mint with sugar (do not use confectioner's sugar). Dip leaves in egg white and then in sugar. Lay on waxed paper to dry. Store in small boxes between layers of waxed paper.

CANDIED SWEET FLAG

Scrape the flag root with great care. Cut in thin slices across root. Boil gently in equal parts of milk and water for 2 hours. Drain well and add to heavy syrup; boil until syrup is absorbed. Place on waxed paper and while hot powder generously with granulated sugar.   Sister Ethel, Sabbathday Lake

Sweet flag is the root of citron grass and is related to the spice Calamus mentioned in the Scriptures. It was used in anointing oils in ancient times. In Europe and in certain parts of this country it is still dug in late fall when thoroughly ripe; the root is scraped, sliced and sugared and eaten as a confection. The North Union Shakers made quantities of this sweetmeat each fall. Sabbathday Lake community still specializes in this quaint sweet.

Angelica is another plant which is candied and used as a sweetmeat (in this case the leaf stock); it is also used for flavoring puddings and sauces. Very delicious.

ROSE HAW PRESERVES

2 CUPS ROSE HAWS (BERRIES OF THE BRIAR ROSE)
1/2 CUP SEEDED RAISINS
1 CUP SUGAR
1 CUP WATER
1/2 TEASPOON ROSEWATER

The rose haw or fruit of the briar rose, which forms in fall after the bloom has gone, is much like the cranberry in appearance. Clip blossom end, and with a very sharp knife remove seeds. Stuff with several raisins. Drop into boiling syrup made by cooking sugar and water. Cook gently about 20 minutes. Add rosewater and seal in very small glass containers. The haws are rare and this preserve is a true and never-to-be-forgotten confection.   Amelia's Shaker Recipes

ROSE PETAL SWEETMEAT

4 CUPS FRESHLY PLUCKED PETALS
4 CUPS WATER
3 1/2 CUPS SUGAR
4 TABLESPOONS STRAINED HONEY
1 TEASPOON LEMON JUICE
DASH OF PINK CAKE COLORING

Cut off the hard base of the rose petals; pack into cup and measure. Put in sauce pan with water and cook 10 minutes. Drain off water and save. Measure one cup rose liquid; add to sugar and honey and cook until it threads from spoon; add lemon juice and cook until petals are transparent. Add just a dash of pink coloring and seal in small glass containers. Very delicious.

CANDIED LOVAGE ROOT

2 CUPS LOVAGE ROOT, SCRAPED AND CUT FINE
6 CUPS WATER
2 CUPS SUGAR
2 CUPS WATER
2 TABLESPOONS SUGAR

Dig the root in the fall when fully ripe; clean by scraping and then cut crosswise. Boil for several hours at low heat, changing water 2 or 3 times. Strain. Boil until clear in heavy syrup, made by cooking sugar and water. Spread on buttered cookie tins and dust well with sugar. Let dry and pack in tin boxes.

Lovage was at one time raised in almost every garden and thus preserved for the winter. Both lovage and sweet flag were considered domestic medicinal remedies, but were used as confections as well. Sabbathday Lake community still makes them.

OLD-FASHIONED HARD CANDY

2 CUPS SUGAR
1/2 CUP MILD VINEGAR
2 TABLESPOONS BUTTER

Mix together and cook until the mixture is hard when tested in cold water. Pour onto a buttered platter and cut into squares while yet warm. When cool enough to handle, roll squares into balls with hands.

SHAKER MINTS

2 CUPS SUGAR
1/2 CUP CORN SYRUP, WHITE
1/2 CUP WATER
1 EGG WHITE, BEATEN
3 DROPS OIL OF PEPPERMINT
3 DROPS GREEN CAKE COLORING

Combine sugar, syrup and water and cook until syrup forms a hard ball when tested in cold water. Beat gradually into the stiffly beaten egg white; add flavoring and coloring and beat until creamy. Drop by spoonfuls on waxed paper.

Sister Mildred Barker, at Sabbathday Lake community, is an excellent candy-maker. Her chocolate mints are considered among the finest made in America.

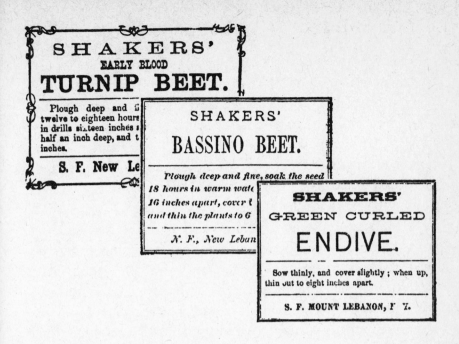

SHAKERS'
EARLY BLOOD
TURNIP BEET.

Plough deep and ⸮⸮
twelve to eighteen hours
in drills sixteen inches ⸮
half an inch deep, and t
inches.

S. F. New Le

SHAKERS'
BASSINO BEET.

Plough deep and fine, soak the seed
18 hours in warm wate
16 inches apart, cover t
and thin the plants to 6

N. F., New Leban

SHAKERS'
GREEN CURLED
ENDIVE.

Sow thinly, and cover slightly ; when up,
thin out to eight inches apart.

S. F. MOUNT LEBANON, N. Y.

Vegetables

The fact that the Shakers were primarily agriculturists, raising not only their grain, vegetables, sugar (maple and honey), fruits, and meats but also their own dairy products, makes their Farm Annals important in the history of American Cookery. Today when dietitians talk alarmingly about the necessity of "the basic seven" and how careful the housewife must be to choose wisely from each of these essential foods, we begin to appreciate what a well-balanced diet the Shakers followed. Depending almost entirely upon the "fat of the land," the Shaker Sisters strove to turn the raw material of their gardens, orchards, cellars and larders into dishes which

239

would give strength and health to the Order and yet would be eaten with real relish and satisfaction by the members. Here in rural Ohio the Shaker records show that lemons and a few spices and an occasional keg of molasses were the only food products purchased from "the world" or outside markets.

Gleanings from their seed catalogs show that their variety of vegetable seeds were legion for that day—endive, six kinds of squash, eight varieties of beans and as many peas, several sorts of both white and yellow sweet corn, melons ranging from luscious water to tiny citrons for preserving. Then we read on about the great cabbage family—red and white varieties, sprouts, kohl, collards, greens of many sorts and mustard in addition to that vast assortment of root vegetables.

Raising this veritable paradise of fresh vegetables along with their assortment of herbs kept the Shakers close to the core of nature. "There is no substitute for keeping fit and young as grubbing in the soil and raising your own victuals," a modern philosopher tells us. In one of the Shaker Farm Journals we read: "Vegetables and fruits, when properly cultivated and prepared as they are freshly gathered, excel in flavor and nourishment. Do not be content with one planting; peas, beans, cucumbers, lettuce, spinach, corn and tomatoes and potatoes should be planted for a constant succession of crops and can be planted as late as the second week in August and yield before the frost sets in. . . ."

As late as 1848 "land scurvy" was still a prevalent disease. Then the medical profession began to realize that the ailment was due to lack of fresh vegetables and fruits in the average diet. Today we know through scientific experiment that fruits and vegetables are rich in minerals and vitamins and essential to good health. As before stated, the Shakers were largely responsible for bringing about a greater use of these necessary foods in the American cuisine.

PARSNIPS

8 MEDIUM PARSNIPS
4 TABLESPOONS BUTTER
2 TABLESPOONS FLOUR
1/2 TEASPOON SALT
1 TEASPOON SUGAR

Scrape parsnips and cut in halves lengthwise. Steam for 45 minutes; this will retain delicate flavor. Dip in melted butter and then in flour and fry in butter. Let them come to a delicate brown and sprinkle with salt and sugar. Serves 6.

North Union

PARSNIP STEW

8 PARSNIPS
6 SMALL POTATOES
WATER
1/4 POUND SALT PORK
SALT AND PEPPER

Cook the parsnips and potatoes with their skins on for 20 minutes. Drain, reserving pot liquor. When cool enough, peel and cut into thick slices. Place in baking dish with thin slices of salt pork. Season with salt and pepper. Fill dish two-thirds with pot-liquor and bake in slow oven (250°) for 30 minutes. Serves 6-8.

Try mashed parsnips for a change. They mash best with a few small potatoes added. Very good!

Parsnips were brought over from Europe and have for centuries been considered a great delicacy. In olden times

241

they were considered poisonous unless they had been frozen. The truth of the matter was that since they were hard to keep in storage they were left in the ground until used. Apparently freezing did not harm their flavor or food value.

ॐ   ঙ্গ

ROASTING EARS OF CORN

Leave the husks on a dozen roasting ears and place them in a slow (300°) oven for 30 minutes. Remove husks and all the silk; serve with plenty of butter and pepper and salt. This is a delicious way to cook corn.   South Union

ॐ   ঙ্গ

BAKED GREENS

2 POUNDS SPINACH, FRESHLY CUT
1/4 POUND SALT PORK
1/2 MEDIUM-SIZED ONION, MINCED
1/4 TEASPOON SALT
1/8 TEASPOON PEPPER
4 POACHED EGGS
DASH OF NUTMEG

Wash spinach four times and pick over carefully. Cut off only roots, for the stems have great food value. Boil, covered, for 15 minutes in water that clings to leaves. Pass through a colander. Try out the salt pork cut in fine pieces and simmer minced onion in fat until tender. Add to spinach with salt and pepper. Turn into serving dish and garnish with poached eggs. Dust with nutmeg. Serves 4.   North Union

ॐ   ঙ্গ

Cress or mustard greens added to spinach greens greatly enhance the flavor.

SHAKER CREAMED POTATOES

1/4 POUND BUTTER
3 CUPS LIGHT CREAM
10 LARGE COLD BOILED POTATOES, SLICED THIN
1 TEASPOON SALT
1/4 TEASPOON PEPPER

Put butter in iron skillet. Melt but do not brown. Add light cream and heat very gently. Drop the sliced potatoes into the cream mixture. Season with salt and pepper. Simmer very slowly until all milk is absorbed. Turn very carefully only once. This takes about an hour. Serve piping hot. Very delicious. Serves 8.   Sister Jennie Wells, Hancock

STUFFED BAKED POTATOES

3 LARGE POTATOES
1 TABLESPOON BUTTER
1/2 TEASPOON SALT
1/8 TEASPOON PEPPER
1/2 CUP CREAM
1 EGG WHITE, BEATEN
DASH OF PAPRIKA

Bake the potatoes in a hot (450°) oven for about 40 minutes. Remove from oven and cut in half lengthwise. Scoop out the inside and pass through a ricer. Add butter, salt, pepper and cream and whip until fluffy. Beat egg white until very stiff and fold into mixture. Pile into shell; dust with paprika and return to oven until golden brown. Serves 6.

Amelia's Shaker Recipes

Although the potato was introduced into Europe in 1553 from South America, it did not become popular in France until 1773, when King Louis XIV, on seeing the plant thrive in the royal garden, wore a potato blossom as a boutonniere. After boiling the leaves and blossoms of this new plant and not finding them very palatable, the King ordered the plant to be uprooted and cast from his garden. It was then they discovered the tuber or potato which has ever since been called the "apple of the earth" in France. The potato soon became a royal delicacy, and many puddings and pastries, as well as vegetable dishes, were concocted from it.

The potato is probably the only vegetable that has a monument dedicated to its discovery! In the town of Hirschhorn stands a memorial thanking "God and Sir Francis Drake, who brought to Europe for the everlasting benefit of the poor, the Potato." This vegetable was originally cultivated in Peru, where it was known to the Indians as the *battata*. In 1553 it was carried to Spain and from thence to Ireland, where it was cultivated on Sir Walter Raleigh's estate near Cork. It became such an important item of diet in Ireland, that it soon became known as the Irish potato. From Ireland it was carried to the North American Colonies.

POTATO SOUFFLÉ

4 MEDIUM POTATOES
1/2 CUP MILK
1/2 CUP BUTTER
1/2 TEASPOON SALT
1/8 TEASPOON PEPPER
2 EGGS, SEPARATED

For full potato flavor boil the potatoes in their jackets. When done, remove skins and pass potatoes through a sieve. Put milk and butter in a saucepan and let come to a full scald; add potato, salt and pepper and beat to a cream. Then add egg yolks and beat well. Beat the whites of eggs and fold into mixture. Turn into a baking dish and bake 20 minutes in a moderate oven (350°). This dish goes well with baked sausage. Serves 4. North Union

An issue of the Shaker *Manifesto* of 1880 contains two columns on, "How to get the most nutriment out of potatoes." Suggestions such as "lay old potatoes in water, if wilted, for half an hour before baking or boiling . . . ; steaming or baking potatoes in their jackets conserves flavor and nourishment. . . . Scrub new potatoes with a stiff brush; boil with their skins and then brown in butter, skins and all. Sprinkle generously with salt and dust with minced chives or parsley; you will find these delicious."

Old Shaker recipe: Pare 6 dozen potatoes of the same size. Set in cold water a few minutes. Place in pot and cover with boiling water and boil rapidly for 20 minutes. Remove cover and add a teaspoon of salt for each dozen potatoes. Cover and cook five minutes longer. Drain off every drop of water and place the pot on the back of the stove. If you are not quite ready to serve potatoes, cover the pot with a light cloth so that the steam can pass off readily, otherwise the potatoes will be dark and soggy and strong in flavor. It takes a mighty good cook to boil a potato to perfection!—Mary Whitcher's *Shaker Housekeeper*

POTATOES IN SHELLS

Bake the needed number of potatoes of equal size. When

245

done, cut in halves lengthwise. Scrape out the interior; mash
and season with salt, pepper and hot cream. Beat until very
fluffy. Return to shell; dot generously with butter and dust
with paprika and minced parsley. Place under broiler until
well heated and brown.   Amelia's Shaker Recipes

SCALLOPED ONIONS

6 MEDIUM ONIONS
4 TABLESPOONS BUTTER
1/3 CUP BREAD CRUMBS
1/2 TEASPOON SALT
1/8 TEASPOON PEPPER
2 TABLESPOONS CREAM
GRATED CHEESE
PAPRIKA

Skin and slice onions. Melt butter and sauté onions in butter
until tender. Place in buttered baking dish, sprinkle with
crumbs, salt and pepper and a little cream. Dust on grated
cheese and a sprinkling of paprika. Bake until crumbs are
brown. Serve very hot. Serves 4.   North Union

A whole book has recently been written on onions. Onions,
leeks, scallions, green onions and shallots all belong to the
onion family. Leeks are for soup—they are milder and more
delicate than the ordinary onion. The white bulbous part is
used in delicate bouillons and in flavoring chicken broth,
while the upper part or green tops are used in flavoring heavy
cream soups and potages such as pea or lentil soups.

Nor must we forget that the lowly onion is a cousin to
the stately lily which graces our gardens.

Science tells us today that the onion is very rich in vitamins B and C. Next to salt and pepper, the onion is the chief seasoner of food. Among the ancient Egyptians, an onion ring was the symbol of everlasting life.

ૢ૰   ૰ૢ

STUFFED ONIONS

6 LARGE SWEET ONIONS
1 CUP VEAL OR CHICKEN, FINELY CHOPPED
1 CUP CELERY, MINCED
2 TABLESPOONS CREAM
1 TEASPOON SALT
1/8 TEASPOON PEPPER
STOCK
1 TABLESPOON BUTTER

Skin onions and boil whole for 10 minutes. Core out centers for stuffing. Make dressing of minced veal, celery, seasoning and cream; stuff in onions. Place in buttered baking dish, moisten with stock and dot with butter. Bake in medium oven (350°) for 20 minutes. (This is a good way to use up soup meat; special seasoning and herbs should be added to soup meats when so utilized.) Serves 6.   Amelia's Shaker Recipes

ૢ૰   ૰ૢ

POOR MAN'S ASPARAGUS

2 POUNDS TENDER GREEN ONIONS
2 TABLESPOONS BUTTER
2 TABLESPOONS FLOUR
1/2 CUP LIGHT CREAM
1 TEASPOON SALT
1/8 TEASPOON PEPPER
2 EGG YOLKS

Remove about 2 inches of tops and boil onions for 10 min-

247

utes. Drain, reserving a cup of pot-liquor. Melt butter and add flour; blend into a smooth paste with the cup of pot-liquor. Add cream, salt and pepper. Arrange onions on hot platter; add cream sauce to beaten yolks of eggs and pour over vegetables. This is a very tasty spring dish. Serves 4-6.

Shaker *Manifesto*

There are sundry articles in the Shaker *Manifesto* on onions. In May, 1880, this magazine carried an article taken from *The Scientific American* on "how cooked or raw onions are among the healthiest of food; colds yield to them like magic and even lung and liver complaints are benefited therefrom. They are cheap and as good a medicine for certain ailments as is within reach. . . ."

Hints: Plant plenty of shallots, green onions, leeks and sweet onions in your garden. They are easy to grow. For each shallot planted you will reap a whole cluster.

SHAKER ASPARAGUS

1 POUND ASPARAGUS TIPS

1 CUP BOILING WATER

1/2 TEASPOON SALT

1/8 TEASPOON SUGAR

2 TABLESPOONS BUTTER

1 SPRIG MINT

1/2 CUP CREAM

2 EGG YOLKS, BEATEN

DASH OF NUTMEG

Break off the tender tops (about 1 inch) from asparagus and set aside. Break remainder in inch lengths (never cut asparagus). Put all except tops in the boiling water; cook 15 minutes. Drain and put in saucepan with seasoning, butter, cream, chopped mint and heads of asparagus. Simmer 10 minutes (do not boil, or cream will curdle). Stir in the beaten egg yolks and simmer just 1 minute. Turn out on buttered toast and sprinkle with nutmeg. Very delicious. Serves 4.

Amelia's Shaker Recipes

The first asparagus was brought to America from Holland in 1786.

Delicately flavored vegetables, such as asparagus, chard or green peas, served with a white sauce are better in flavor if sauce is made of half milk and half water in which vegetable has been cooked. Thickened milk and cream are often too heavy and destroy the flavor of the food. Asparagus was called "sparrow grass" in olden times; it greatly resembles the garden lily when it first pokes its head through the soil in early spring. When it is only half an inch high is the time to cut it with a long sharp knife down several inches below the surface. It is then very tender and bleached.—Shaker Recipes

SHAKER SQUASH

4 POUNDS HUBBARD SQUASH
1 CUP HOT WATER
1/2 TEASPOON SALT
1/2 TEASPOON PEPPER
3 TABLESPOONS BUTTER
1/2 CUP MAPLE SYRUP

Steam or bake the squash in the hot water. Remove from shell when tender; pass through sieve and season with salt, pepper, butter and maple syrup. Beat well and heat before serving. Serves 6.

Or

Put a whole hubbard squash in a slow oven and bake for 2 1/2 hours. Remove. It will now cut easily. Remove seeds and fiber. Divide into serving portions, place in pan and dust well with salt, pepper and brown sugar and dot heavily with butter. Set under broiler to brown. Any remaining squash can be used for pies or puddings in place of pumpkin.

Summer squash may be steamed or boiled, but do not pare or remove seeds. When tender pass through coarse sieve and season well with salt, pepper, plenty of butter and a little cream. Place in buttered baking dish and let brown on top.

Today squash has come into its own; it is souffléd, baked, mashed, stuffed, pan-broiled, concocted into puddings and delectable puffs and pies.

SISTER LUELLA'S TOMATO FRITTERS

2 CUPS THICK TOMATO PURÉE

1 1/2 CUP FINE CRACKER CRUMBS

2 TABLESPOONS ONION, MINCED

1 1/2 TEASPOONS SUGAR

1 TABLESPOON FLOUR

1/2 TEASPOON SALT

1/8 TEASPOON PEPPER
3 EGGS
3 TABLESPOONS BUTTER

Mix all ingredients except eggs and butter. Beat eggs well and add to mixture. Heat butter in skillet and drop in fritters by spoonfuls. Fry to a delicate brown. Good! Serves 4-6.

In an eastern Shaker Journal we read: "Tomatoes were called 'love apples' and were used only as ornamental shrubs in gardens until 1815, when Dr. Burnett, a teacher in a medical school, pronounced the tomato a valuable food. He went so far as to say this fruit should be eaten daily in one form or another. He recommended that tomatoes be used where the need of calomel is indicated; he claimed tomatoes are just as effective in such cases and absolutely harmless. We are now growing this valuable food in great profusion."

The tomato seed was brought from South America to Spain shortly after the discovery of the New World. The fruit at that time was very small. Through many decades of cultivation as an ornamental plant the fruit developed into a succulent food. It is probably the most universally eaten vegetable in the world today. No restaurant or hotel is without a can of tomatoes in some form!

The Shaker *Manifesto* ran many articles on the healthful properties of the tomato; countless recipes were published, and probably not a day went by at North Union and other communities that tomatoes were not served in some shape or form ranging from fritters to soups, to custards, to condiments!

SHAKER STRING BEANS

2 POUNDS GREEN BEANS
1/4 POUND SALT PORK, CHOPPED
PINCH OF SODA
1 TEASPOON SUGAR
1/2 TEASPOON SALT
DASH OF PEPPER
1/2 CUP CREAM

Break off ends of beans and break into 2-inch lengths. Soak in cold water for 10 minutes. Try out salt pork in bottom of pot; when slightly browned add beans and a cup of boiling water. When boiling add a very small amount soda and cook for 20 minutes. Drain off water; add sugar, salt, pepper and cream and simmer for 5 minutes. Keep very hot.

For the fine variety of beans we enjoy in America today, we are indebted to the American Indian. The soy (Chinese) bean, the lima and the broad bean were all known to the Old World before Columbus made his discovery. Here he found several species of beans extensively raised by the natives. From these many of our varieties have been developed.

Many of the vegetables and herbs we cultivate and eat today were used strictly for medicinal purposes by the Greek and Egyptian physicians. . . . Peas, beans, lentils and cucumbers were known in very ancient times. However, vegetables did not become a part of the daily diet of the common people until the latter part of the eighteenth century. Meat, cheese, bread and beer were the staple diet of the poor until that date.

Special Diet for Aged

Of all the tons of meat the Shaker Sisters cured, dried, jerked and smoked, of all the thousands of gallons of applesauce they painstakingly made for home and "world" consumption —none of their cookery efforts were as significant as the special diets and dishes they prepared for the aging members of their communities!

Among the Shakers there was no fixed age limit for retirement—no deadline of usefulness. In fact, there was no distinct class of dependent old folks among them, for the genuine affection and respect in which they held their "ripening saints," whose years had been spent in unselfish devotion in serving others, changed the "blight of old age to the glory of harvest"! The Shakers were very advanced in their attitude toward ripening years, for they believed in every member—both old and young—working according to his strength and ability. They considerately lightened the load of their older members but never robbed them of their sense of usefulness. Often, even when strength is lessened, the individual's judgment and experience may still be of more value than ever, and he or she should not be thrust aside. Psychologists tell us today that "the deadline of usefulness" is dreaded far more than death by the aged! Among the Shakers no one was faced with anxiety and grim forebodings of a lonely, deserted old age. Moreover, the Shaker's wholesome conception of death as a beginning of a new and more abundant life kept his eyes bright and his step light. Life to him was never a solemn march down into the grave but a lilting step up to celestial fields rife with new adventures.

Even in extreme old age, no Shaker was ever thrust outside the interests of the home; as their steps slackened they advanced to honorary posts such as consulting new members, training them, visiting the sick and needy in the vicinity, or making frequent visits to the school. These light chores gave new interests and purpose to their lives.

Again, the Shakers warded off many of the disabilities of old age by furnishing especially nutritive diets for those over sixty. Today many of the ailments of senility are laid at the door of chronic undernourishment—especially a lack of the right kind of food. We have believed in the past that with advancing years, the individual needed less nutritious food, that the aged should "eat lightly." Often this led to a high starch diet which resulted in overweight, putting an undue burden upon the heart and circulatory system. Again, faulty teeth have led to meatless diet. This, too, is a mistake, for the aging need meat, poultry, eggs, and fish and milk products. As bones become brittle with old age, the same amount of calcium as is given to children is needed—a quart of milk a day consumed in various ways is the rule. Nor can we neglect the vitamins and minerals in the diets of the old!

Through sheer reverence and parental love the Shakers hit upon very adequate diets for their members over sixty. Soups, stews and broths, laden with vitamins, minerals and proteins, made of red beef, liver and kidneys, etc., were given them. Also plenty of greens and fruits, great quantities of tomatoes, ample butter, milk, cheese and eggs went into the specially prepared foods for the aged and the sick. The Shakers realized that as a person became less active, he should omit heavy, rich foods and should have the simple, easily digested food fed to children. This the Shaker Sisters achieved.

Today we know it is the condition of our arteries and not calendars which determine our life span. Science, also, tells us that "tissue breakdown in the aging is not caused by nutritional lacks alone but by the psychological factors as well"—the feeling of being left out of things! Due to the high cost of living and living in one- or two-room apartments, many parents are shelved away in homes for the aged where they are almost isolated from life. This never happened in the Shaker communities where the rich wisdom of the aging members, their ripening attitude toward life, was sought after and cherished by the younger of the large families.

DELICATE SHAKER OMELET

1 TABLESPOON FLOUR

1 CUP WARM MILK

6 EGG YOLKS, BEATEN

1/2 TEASPOON SALT

6 EGG WHITES, BEATEN

2 TABLESPOONS SOFT BUTTER

Moisten flour with a little milk and stir into warm milk. Add beaten egg yolks and salt and stir until smooth. Beat egg whites and fold into batter. Turn into a buttered baking dish and bake 25 minutes in a slow (300°) oven. Serves 4.

CHICKEN GELATIN

2 TABLESPOONS GELATIN

1/4 CUP COLD WATER

2 CUPS CHICKEN STOCK (SEE INDEX)

1/2 TEASPOON SALT

1/8 TEASPOON PAPRIKA

3 HARD-COOKED EGGS

1 TABLESPOON PARSLEY, MINCED

3 CUPS COOKED CHICKEN, SLICED

Pour gelatin on cold water and let stand 5 minutes. Heat chicken stock and dissolve gelatin in it. Add salt, if necessary, and paprika. Pour 1/2 cup gelatin into a flat pan. Let harden. Slice eggs and arrange on set gelatin, and sprinkle with minced parsley. Add 1/8 cup gelatin mixture (just enough to hold eggs and parsley). Let harden. Then add chicken to mixture and pour into mold. Chill until set and turn out on a platter. This dish is both delicious and pleasing to the eye. Serves 6.   Sister Lisset

256

BEEF TEA

1 POUND PRIME LEAN BEEF, CHOPPED
1/2 TEASPOON SALT
DASH OF PEPPER
1 1/2 CUPS WATER
A FEW SPRIGS PARSLEY

Put chopped meat in top of double boiler, add salt and pepper and water and let stand for 2 hours; this will slowly draw out the nourishment. Simmer for 2 hours. Add parsley last half hour. Strain and chill. Remove any fat from top when cold.   Eldress Clymena

SISTER LOTTIE'S CHICKEN SOUP

4 POUND HEN, CUT UP
2 1/2 QUARTS WATER
1 SMALL ONION, MINCED
2 STALKS ANISE, MINCED
1 BAY LEAF, WHOLE
6 PEPPERCORNS
1 TEASPOON SALT
2/3 CUP RICE, UNCOOKED
1 TABLESPOON PARSLEY, MINCED

Simmer chicken for 3 hours. Remove from bones and cut in cubes. Add onion, anise, bay leaf, peppercorns, salt and washed rice to broth; cook slowly until rice is tender. Remove bay leaf and peppercorns and add cubed chicken and parsley. Heat thoroughly and serve. Serves 6.

CALF'S FOOT JELLY

4 CALF'S FEET
2 QUARTS WATER
1/3 CUP SUGAR
3 EGG WHITES, SLIGHTLY BEATEN
JUICE OF 1 LEMON
1 TEASPOON SALT
1 PINT WHITE WINE
DASH OF NUTMEG AND MACE

Thoroughly cleanse the calf's feet and boil slowly until meat separates from the bones. Strain the liquid into an earthen crock with straight sides. When the liquid has jelled, turn it from the crock; scrape all fat from top and all sediment from bottom of jelly. Heat and add sugar, the slightly beaten egg whites, lemon juice, salt and white wine along with a dash of nutmeg and mace. Stir well and let come to boil. Then pass through sieve lined with several thicknesses of cheesecloth. By no means squeeze cloth, for that would cloud the jelly. Jelly of this kind is most useful in the diet of the aged and for children, let alone the sick room. No kitchen should be without it. An endless variety of dishes can be concocted from this base: cooked meats, fish, vegetables, fruits and even creamed or grated cheese can be added in many combinations which make attractive and easily eaten nutriment.

Sister Melissa, Watervliet, Ohio

ह𝔴   ᘿᔍ

Today we use packaged gelatin; the early Shakers made their own.

ह𝔴   ᘿᔍ

258

MOLDED FRUIT SALAD

2 CUPS CALF'S FOOT JELLY *or*
1 PACKAGE LEMON GELATIN, DISSOLVED
    IN 2 CUPS HOT WATER
2 CUPS CANNED PEARS, DICED
2 CUPS CANNED PEACHES, DICED
1/2 CUP WHITE GRAPES
1 TABLESPOON ORANGE MARMALADE

Either melt calf's foot jelly and cool, or add hot water to gelatin and let cook. Add well-drained and diced canned fruit, grapes and marmalade and pour into mold to harden. Serve with favorite dressing.

JELLIED VEAL

4 VEAL SHANKS, SPLIT
2 QUARTS WATER
1/8 TEASPOON PEPPER
1 TEASPOON SALT
1 BAY LEAF
1 BLADE OF MACE
2 STALKS CELERY, MINCED
8 SPRIGS PARSLEY, MINCED
1 CARROT, COOKED AND MINCED
1 TABLESPOON GREEN PEPPER, MINCED
1 TEASPOON CHERVIL, CUT

Boil the split veal shanks with the seasoning slowly for 3 hours. Separate the meat and tear into shreds. When the pot-liquor is cold, strain until clear and pour over meat in mold to which the minced vegetables and herbs have been added. Chill until jellied. This can be cut into slices and served on a

259

bed of lettuce leaves as a salad or served as a cold meat. It is a very nourishing dish.   Old Canterbury

ट॰   ॰ई

CHICKEN POT PIE

1 RECIPE BISCUIT DOUGH (SEE INDEX)
1 COOKED CHICKEN, BONED
6 SMALL RAW POTATOES, PEELED AND SLICED VERY
    FINE
2 CUPS RAW SHELLED PEAS
SALT AND PEPPER
4 SPRIGS MARJORAM, MINCED
4 SPRIGS PARSLEY, MINCED
3 CUPS LIGHT CREAM
2 EGGS, BEATEN

Line the sides but not the bottom of a baking dish with your best biscuit crust. Place in bottom a layer of cooked chicken which has had bones and skin removed. Cover with a layer of raw sliced potatoes and sprinkle with raw peas, salt and pepper. Lay a few very thin strips of dough across and sprinkle with herbs. Repeat layers until pan is three-quarters filled. Then season light cream and add well-beaten eggs and pour over layers. Put on a thin top crust, allowing a steam vent. Bake in a moderate (350°) oven for 45 minutes.

Amelia's Shaker Recipes

ट॰   ॰ई

BAKED BEEF TONGUE

1 BEEF TONGUE
2 CUPS TOMATOES, CUT UP
1 SMALL ONION, DICED

3 STALKS CELERY, CUT FINE
1/2 TEASPOON SALT
DASH OF PEPPER

Boil tongue in salted water until tender (about 2 hours).
When cool enough, peel and cut out root. Place in a baking
dish with tomatoes, onion, celery, salt and dash of pepper.
Add 1/2 cup pot-liquor and simmer for 45 minutes. Thicken
sauce with corn or potato flour. This is a tender and easily
digested food and, in addition, is very nourishing.

Shaker *Manifesto*

KIDNEY AND STEAK PIE

4 VEAL KIDNEYS
GOOD BISCUIT DOUGH FOR 2 CRUSTS (SEE INDEX)
1 CUP RAW ROAST BEEF, CUBED
1 CUP RAW POTATOES, SLICED
2 HARD-COOKED EGGS
1 CUP POT-LIQUOR
SALT AND PEPPER

Remove all fiber and excess fat from kidneys. Soak overnight
in water. Boil slowly in same water until tender. Remove kidneys; save water. Cut kidneys into thin slices. Line a well-
buttered deep baking dish with a thin layer of biscuit dough.
(Some prefer pie dough for this dish.) Put in layers of kidneys, beef, sliced potatoes and sliced egg. Repeat until ingredients are used up. Pour over it the liquor in which the kidneys were cooked, and season. Cover with dough and bake in
a hot (450°) oven until richly browned, about 40 minutes.
Serves 6.   Mary Whitcher's *Shaker Housekeeper*

SHAKER SWEETBREADS

1 PAIR SWEETBREADS, VEAL OR LAMB
2 TABLESPOONS BUTTER
2 TABLESPOONS FLOUR
SWEETBREAD BROTH
1 TABLESPOON LEMON JUICE
1/2 TEASPOON SALT
DASH OF PEPPER
2 EGG YOLKS
1 TABLESPOON PARSLEY, MINCED

Parboil sweetbreads in slightly salted water; drain, reserving broth. Carefully trim off all fat and membrane. Cut in half-inch squares. Make a white sauce by melting butter and blending in flour; add 2 cups of sweetbread broth. Flavor with lemon juice and taste for need of salt. Add pepper. Just before serving, beat up egg yolks thinned with a bit of broth and add to sauce. Add sweetbreads. Serve on rounds of hot buttered toast and sprinkle with parsley. Serve immediately. Green peas should be served with this dish. Serves 4.

"Only veal, lamb or mutton sweetbreads are used in cookery. They are a great delicacy and should be enjoyed more often. All the viscera, heart, kidneys, liver, tripe and sweetbreads are highly nutritious and can be made into very inviting dishes with a little thought and care."—Sister Lottie

BROILED SWEETBREADS

2 PAIRS SWEETBREADS, VEAL OR LAMB
4 CUPS COLD WATER
1/2 TEASPOON SALT
JUICE OF 1/2 LEMON

2 TABLESPOONS MELTED BUTTER

Lay sweetbreads in cold water for an hour, changing water several times. Then cover with cold water to which salt and lemon juice have been added. Simmer 15 minutes. Again lay in cold water to bleach. Remove membrane. Place between 2 platters and weight top platter to flatten meat. Broil with butter and season delicately. This is excellent food for the aged or for children. Serves 4-6.

ॐ   ॐ

"Never buy tripe from the market, but get it fresh from the slaughter house or use very fresh when butchering at home. It is a part of the third stomach of the cow. When well cooked it is very tender and delicious. It must be cooked slowly and thoroughly. Scrape the tripe with the dull edge of a knife and keep wiping with a dry cloth. Never subject tripe to water, for it is very porous and takes up water readily. Have a skillet medium hot and use half lard and half butter and fry very slowly to a delicate brown. Serve immediately. Do not season with anything; not even salt!"—Sister Lisett

ॐ   ॐ

BAKED LIVER WITH ONIONS

1 BERMUDA ONION, SLICED

2 TABLESPOONS BUTTER

1/4 CUP HOT WATER

6 SLICES VEAL OR LAMB LIVER

2 TABLESPOONS FLOUR, SEASONED WITH SALT AND
    PEPPER

1 BAY LEAF

8 SPRIGS PARSLEY

2 SPRIGS THYME

Place slices of Bermuda onion in a well-buttered baking dish.

Melt butter in hot water and pour over onion. Cover and bake 30 minutes at 350°. Remove tubes and skin from liver and dredge slices with seasoned flour; arrange over onions in baking dish. Add herbs tied with kitchen thread, and dot with butter. Bake covered for 30 minutes at 350°; uncover and bake until liver is browned.

ॐ   ॐ

"Food experts claim liver is a real blood-builder and that it furnishes quick energy. We try to serve it to our sick and aged at least once a week. Beef, pork, poultry and game liver are equally healthy but are best made into dressing, sausage, loaves and fillings."

ॐ   ॐ

TOMATO CUSTARD

4 POUNDS RIPE TOMATOES
4 EGGS, BEATEN
1 CUP MILK
1/2 CUP SUGAR
1/2 TEASPOON SALT
1/8 TEASPOON NUTMEG

Stew tomatoes in own juice (no water used) and pass through sieve. Cool and add to beaten eggs, milk and seasoning. Bake in buttered custard cups. Serves 6.

ॐ   ॐ

SISTER ABIGAIL'S STRAWBERRY FLUMMERY

2 1/4 CUPS MILK, SCALDED
3/4 CUP MILK
1/3 CUP CORNSTARCH

264

2 TABLESPOONS SUGAR

1/4 TEASPOON SALT

1 EGG, BEATEN

1/2 TEASPOON ROSEWATER OR VANILLA

1 QUART FRESH STRAWBERRIES, HULLED AND CRUSHED

4 TABLESPOONS SUGAR

Scald milk; add cold milk and stir well. Mix cornstarch, sugar and salt; moisten with milk and stir into heated milk. Cook over very low flame, or in double boiler, until mixture thickens. Beat egg well, add sugar and flavoring and add hot mixture to egg mixture, beating it and returning to low fire for 2 minutes. Pour into mold or dish. Chill, turn out and cover with strawberries well crushed and sweetened. Red raspberries or loganberries can be substituted for strawberries. Serves 6.

CHOCOLATE SOUFFLÉ

2 TABLESPOONS BUTTER

3 TABLESPOONS FLOUR

1 CUP MILK

2 OUNCES UNSWEETENED CHOCOLATE

1 TABLESPOON SUGAR

1/4 TEASPOON SALT

2 TABLESPOONS BOILING WATER

3 EGG YOLKS, BEATEN

1/2 TEASPOON VANILLA

3 EGG WHITES, BEATEN

3 TABLESPOONS STRAWBERRY JAM

Melt butter, add flour and blend well; gradually add milk and heat to boiling point. Melt chocolate in top of double boiler and add sugar, salt and boiling water. Blend and combine the two mixtures. Pour over well-beaten egg yolks, and add vanilla. Beat egg whites until very stiff and fold into mixture. Butter baking dish and spread bottom with half-inch layer of strawberry jam. Pour on soufflé and bake in 350° oven for 35 minutes. Serve with plain cream. Serves 4.

ફ્રે   ક્ર્ે

ROSEWATER ICE CREAM

1 1/2 CUPS MILK
3 EGG YOLKS
3/4 CUP SUGAR
1/8 TEASPOON SALT
1 PINT HEAVY CREAM, WHIPPED
1/2 TABLESPOON ROSEWATER (SEE INDEX)

Scald milk over a low flame; add to this the beaten egg yolks mixed with sugar and salt. Cook very slowly until slightly thick. Chill thoroughly. Add rosewater and fold in the heavy cream. Do not use cream less than a day old. Place mixture in freezer and turn until it thickens. Remove dasher and pack and let stay for several hours. This is always a favorite dessert, especially among the older ones and the children. Serves 4.

ફ્રે   ક્ર્ે

After the North Union Shakers built their ice-house in 1874 and cut and stored their own ice, ice cream was a common dessert among them. Like their butter churns of that date, they had their freezer driven by water power in the dairy. "Good home-made ice cream for supper" is an entry found in several of the visiting Elders' journals.

Ice cream, which is by far the most popular dessert in America today, originated in Italy when an ingenious cook sent to the Italian mountains for ice in order to prepare a great delicacy for Catherine De'Medici (1514-89). When this renowned lady became Queen of France, she carried this cherished recipe with her.

Dolly Madison was credited with introducing ice cream to the United States, when she served it at a White House dinner in 1808. So popular did this confection become, that the cook who made it for the mistress of the White House resigned soon after and set himself up as "An Ice Cream Specialist."

LIGHT CAKE

1/2 CUP BUTTER

1 CUP SUGAR

2 EGGS

2 CUPS MILK

3 CUPS FLOUR, SIFTED

3 TEASPOONS BAKING POWDER

1/2 TEASPOON ROSEWATER, OR OTHER FLAVORING

Cream butter and sugar together. Add beaten eggs. Alternately add the milk and dry ingredients, sifted together, in small quantities, until well mixed. Add flavoring and bake in loaf pan in moderate (350°) oven for 35 minutes.

GRAPE JUICE ICE

2 CUPS WATER

1 CUP SUGAR

1/8 TEASPOON SALT

1 TABLESPOON GELATIN

2 CUPS BOTTLED GRAPE JUICE

1/2 CUP LEMON JUICE

GRATED RIND OF 1/2 ORANGE

267

Make a syrup of water, sugar and salt. Dissolve gelatin in a little cold water and add to syrup. Add juices and rind, and cool. Freeze in ice cream mixer until mushy. Pack and let freeze. Very refreshing.

ॐ   ॐ

Custards, snows, eggnogs, fish and egg dishes, tomatoes in twenty ways, all the leafy vegetables and stewed and fresh fruits were part of the Shakers' old-age diet. Even during the ban on meat-eating, the rule did not apply to those members over sixty. Much of this special diet was "minced, diced, ground, hacked or hewed," which made the food easy to eat and digest for those who had tooth trouble in a day when dentistry was not widely employed.

Whole wheat and breads made from other unbolted flour were fed to the older members. The Shakers were seriously opposed to bolting wheat which took out the very elements which are required to build nerves, muscles, bone and brain. Today we again demand "enriched flours"—even our government requires it.

In the *Manifesto* of November, 1880, we read: "Our bodies are the food we eat. There are definite laws of nutrition which should be studied and followed rather than man eating to please his palate. . . . When our meals are disturbed by anger, passion, hate or even haste we develop bodily disorders. . . . All our meals should be eaten calmly and deliberately and as pleasantly as possible. . . . When we Americans learn the great lesson that all Life is a Unit; that the physical, intellectual and the spiritual are all One Life and that whatever mars one phase of it mars the whole—we will be far better off."

Gather up the Fragments

One fine Saturday morning in August, 1782, Mother Ann and the Elders, with a large company of Believers, set forth from the Goodrich home at Hancock to visit New Lebanon. It is recorded that they arrived at Israel Talcott's place atop the mountain shortly before noon. Here they were warmly received. Abigail Talcott had her pot of meat and vegetables over the fire preparing dinner for her little family. Mother Ann spoke to Abigail, saying, "We have need of food; you must feed us, Abigail, and all who are with us."

To this Abigail Talcott answered, "Yea! But I must cook more meat and sauce."

"Nay! There is plenty!" responded Mother Ann.

Accordingly, Abigail took up her dinner, and all the company consisting of nearly forty persons sat down and ate and were amply satisfied. Abigail was greatly astonished that such a host could be fed and satisfied upon so small a quantity of victuals. "At the meeting which followed so great was the manifestation of the power of God and so clear the evidence of the testimony that every mouth was stopped!"

This miraculous feeding of hosts of followers was often repeated when Mother Ann and her little band traveled about the eastern countryside visiting possible converts and constantly gathering in new ones. This devout leader realized full well that "man does not live by bread alone," and satisfied their hunger, often after traveling miles on foot, by feeding them crumbs of truth so abundantly furnished by the Master.

In her youth Mother Ann had seen lack of food and dire need among the poor in the rapidly growing milltown of Manchester, which led her to abhor waste of all kinds. Her followers who organized the Shaker Church and the various communities laid down rules to prevent waste. One of these was: "Nothing edible is to be left upon the plate when a Shaker has finished his meal." He could help himself as often as he wished so long as he ate what he had taken. Even strangers who dined with the Shakers were expected to conform in this matter. Lest there be a misunderstanding about it, a set of printed rules was posted in the dining halls. This Table Monitor, as it was called, was written by Sister Hannah Bronson, a native of Vermont who entered the Mt. Lebanon community in 1800.

TABLE MONITOR

"Gather up the fragments, that nothing be lost."

Here there is the pattern which Jesus Christ has set,
And his good example we cannot forget;
With thanks for his blessing, his word we'll obey
But on this occasion we have something to say.

We wish to speak plainly and use no deceit;
We like to see fragments left wholesome and neat;
To customs and fashions we make no pretense,
Yet think we can tell what belongs to good sense.

What we deem goodly order we're willing to state,
Eat hearty and decent, and clean out our plate;
Be thankful to heaven for what we receive
And not make a mixture or compound to leave.

We find of those bounties which heaven does give,
That some live to eat, and that some eat to live;
That some think of nothing but pleasing the taste
And care very little how much they do waste,

Though heaven has blessed us with plenty of food,
Bread, butter and honey, and all that is good;
We loathe to see mixtures where gentlefolk dine,
Which scarcely look fit for the poultry and swine.

We often find left on the same China dish
Meat, applesauce, pickle, brown bread and minced fish;
Another replenished with butter and cheese,
With pie, cake and toast, perhaps added to these.

Now if any virtue in this can be shown
By peasant, by lawyer, or king on the throne,
We freely will forfeit whatever we've said
And call it a virtue to waste meat and bread.

Let none be offended at what we here say,
We candidly ask you, is that the best way?
If not, lay such customs and fashions aside,
And this Monitor take henceforth for your guide.

The term "Shaker your plate" is commonly used, and comes from this custom of not taking more food than one wishes to eat—waste nothing!

Perhaps we Americans need a little "Shakering of our plates" today. Some modern food authorities claim that Americans waste from 20% to 30% of the food we produce annually; that these losses occur in harvesting, shipping, storing and in our use of food: that one fourth of this appalling loss takes place in the home where the average American family wastes 400 pounds of food a year—by over-buying, by preparing food poorly, by leaving it upon our plates and by spoilage in improper storage.

It is little wonder that the Shakers were appalled at this sinful waste when hungry wayfarers constantly asked for bread at their hospitable gates! In a letter from Elder Matthew Houston at North Union to the Ministry at Mt. Lebanon he stated: "Daily there are demands made upon us for food. Due to the bad weather there is a grave shortage of wheat in these parts; this means that many are hungry. So far we have not sent away any without bread. . . ." Again it is recorded that during the financial depression of 1873 more than four thousand meals were given to the unemployed who sought relief at Union Village.

Today's leaders in the conservation of food again ask us

to "Shaker our plates," for they claim that if each family wastes only a single slice of bread daily it means 34,000,000 slices across the nation—over 2,000,000 loaves of bread daily relegated to the garbage can at a cost of $320,000 daily! Again, these experts tell us to use all edible parts of food, such as beet and turnip tops when fresh, leaves of celery and tops of onions and to use our garden vegetables as freshly gathered as possible. All this economy was strictly practiced by the Shakers a hundred or more years ago—long before anything was known about vitamins and minerals. Simply for economy's sake, they salvaged all edible greens, pot-liquors, skins of fruit and peels of vegetables, thus gleaning much valuable nutrition. They used the bones and trimmings of meat, fish and fowl for broth in re-enforcing stews, gravies and soups. They made excellent use of all leftovers. They made all excess milk into cheese. When certain recipes called for large quantities of egg yolks, they immediately concocted dishes which used up the corresponding whites. Their minute care in storing food properly was another tremendous item in conservation of food. Their Household Journals are replete with warnings: "Ventilate your storage places and cellars well. . . . Constantly watch the brine on your pickle . . . on your salt meats. . . . Assort your apples frequently, for one bad one will contaminate the whole barrel. . . ."

Today we are told that our desire for food is closely related to our emotions—that almost any emotional disturbance affects our appetites and also our digestions, and that many of the stomach ulcers are due to our haste and anxious mode of living. The wise Shakers foresaw all this; they condemned haste in eating, haste in living. They understood the necessity of making mealtime a joyous time—a time of satisfaction and contentment. In a little manual gotten out by the Shakers in 1823, entitled *Gentle Manners,* we read some wise statements, such as: "It is necessary at table that we consider

273

the happiness of those about us, therefore a system of rules must be observed during the time occupied at table in order to make it a pleasurable satisfaction as well as a physical necessity. . . . Remember that a slight deviation from the rules of good manners at table may offend those about us so that the meal becomes an occasion of pain instead of pleasure. . . . Sit erect at table, inclining the body slightly forward in order to be close to your food. . . . Keep your arms near your body—never on the table. Also be careful to have your feet directly in front of your own chair, never in the way of others. . . . Remember there is a proper way to use knife, fork and spoon as well as napkin. . . . Neither eat nor drink in haste and carefully avoid making any noises while eating. . . . Our lives are primarily for the purpose of giving pleasure to others, to those about us, therefore we must practice orderliness and cleanliness—without which we are not worthy of the name gentleman or Christian. . . . Be not angry or sour at table; whatever may happen put on a cheerful mien, for good humor makes one dish a feast. . . ."

Today food is not a matter of cook books telling of new flavors to stimulate and appease jaded appetites or taste buds, but is the subject for grave national and international conferences on conservation and distribution of food. All the wise laws the United Nations can shape into constitutions and charters will never establish universal peace so long as there are nations where starvation and malnutrition are vital problems. The forces of hunger are mighty! "Freedom from Want" is written in calories. Nutrition, population controls, a wider scope for the aged and a practical brotherhood among God's children are the burning issues of today and tomorrow. The humble Shakers answered all their problems by listening constantly to the "still, small voice." They have set before our nation, yea, before the world, an example of 178 years of practical Christian living.

INDEX

INDEX

Herbs *(cont'd)*
 rosewater, 132
 sage, 129, 133
 Shaker stuffing for chicken,
  130
 string bean salad, 128
 thyme, 125, 131
hoarhound candy, 234
hog's head cheese, 138
hominy cakes, Shaker, 78
horseradish sauce, 112
huckleberry muffins, Sister Hattie's, 53

ice cream, rosewater, 266
icings, cake, 62
India relish, 190
Indian griddle cakes, 83
Indian pudding, Shaker, 92

jam,
 sour cherry, 198
 strawberry, 197
 tomato, 202
jelly,
 apple parings, 195
 peach, Sister Lettie's, 196
Jennie, Sister, 50
Johnny cake, Shaker, 76

kidney and steak pie, 261

lamb, roast leg of, 149
lemon,
 beer, Shaker, 30
 cake sauce, 67
 pie, 172
  Ohio, 173
lemonade, Shaker-style, 29
lentil loaf, 161
Lettie, Sister, 68, 148, 169, 174, 196, 208
Lisset, Sister, 49, 52

liver, baked with onions, 263
Lizzie, Sister, 178
Lottie, Sister, 51, 170
lovage root, candied, 237
Luella, Sister, 219, 250

maple,
 cream candy, 234
 pie, Sister Lettie's, 174
 sugar cake, 63
marjoram, 125, 130
marmalade, carrot, 202
Meat, 135-152
 bacha brine, 151
 corned beef and cabbage, 143
 dumplings, 145
 guinea hen, roasted, 146
 ham baked in cider, 144
 pork roast, 140
 Shaker beef stew, 144
 Shaker flank steak, 139
 Shaker fried chicken, 147
 Shaker hog's head cheese, 138
 Shaker roast leg of lamb, 149
 Sister Clymena's chicken pie, 150
 Sister Content's hash, 142
 Sister Lettie's veal loaf, 148
 venison roast, 145
 wild turkey roasted, 141
Meatless Dishes, 153-166
 cheese omelet, 164
 chestnut omelet, 159
 lentil loaf, 161
 mushrooms and chestnuts, 156
 nut and rice patties, 157
 Shaker baked beans, 158
 Shaker cheese balls, 163
 Shaker cheese soufflé, 165
 Shaker dolmas, 163
 Shaker rarebit, 160
mincemeat for pies, 172
mint, 125, 133